Smocking with Ribbon

A New Pleasure

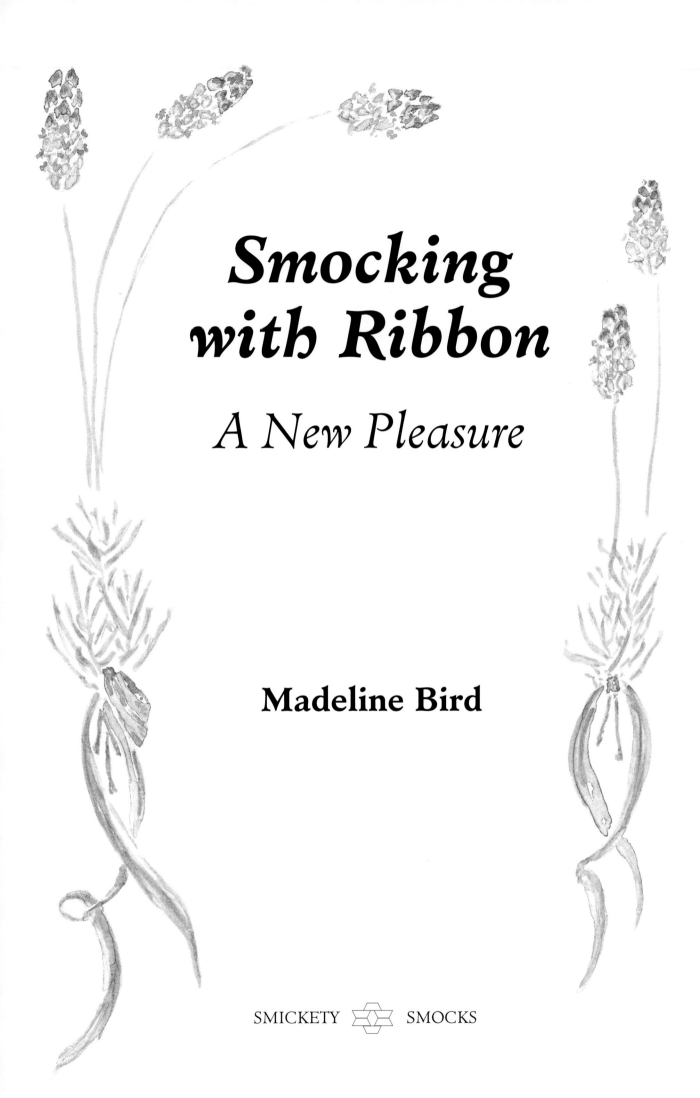

Smocking with Ribbon

A New Pleasure

Madeline Bird

SMICKETY SMOCKS

First published 1993
Second Edition 1994
Published by: Smickety Smocks
P.O. Box 138
Newlands 7725 R.S.A.
© Text. Graphics and Photographs: Madeline Bird 1993
All rights reserved.
The moral right of the author has been asserted.
ISBN 0—620—17330—0

Designed and Typeset by:	Jo Worthington-Smith DTP Design cc, Cape Town
Graphic Drawings by:	Jo Worthington-Smith DTP Design cc, Cape Town
Photography by:	Nicholas Hymns
Reproduction by:	Hirt & Carter and Nasionale Pers
Printed and Bound by:	Printed and Bound in Singapore by Kyodo Printing Co.
Distributed by:	David Philip Publishers (Pty) Ltd. Cape Town
	Creative Smocking, Portland, Oregon, U.S.A.

Patterns for the garments that appear in this book are available from:
SMICKETY SMOCKS
P. O. Box 138
Newlands 7725
Fax: (021) 683-4160

Dedication

*To Ron Bird, whose wonderful
zest for living will always be an inspiration.
Thank you for believing in me.*

*To Auntie Girlie Smith,
for loving me as the daughter she never had.*

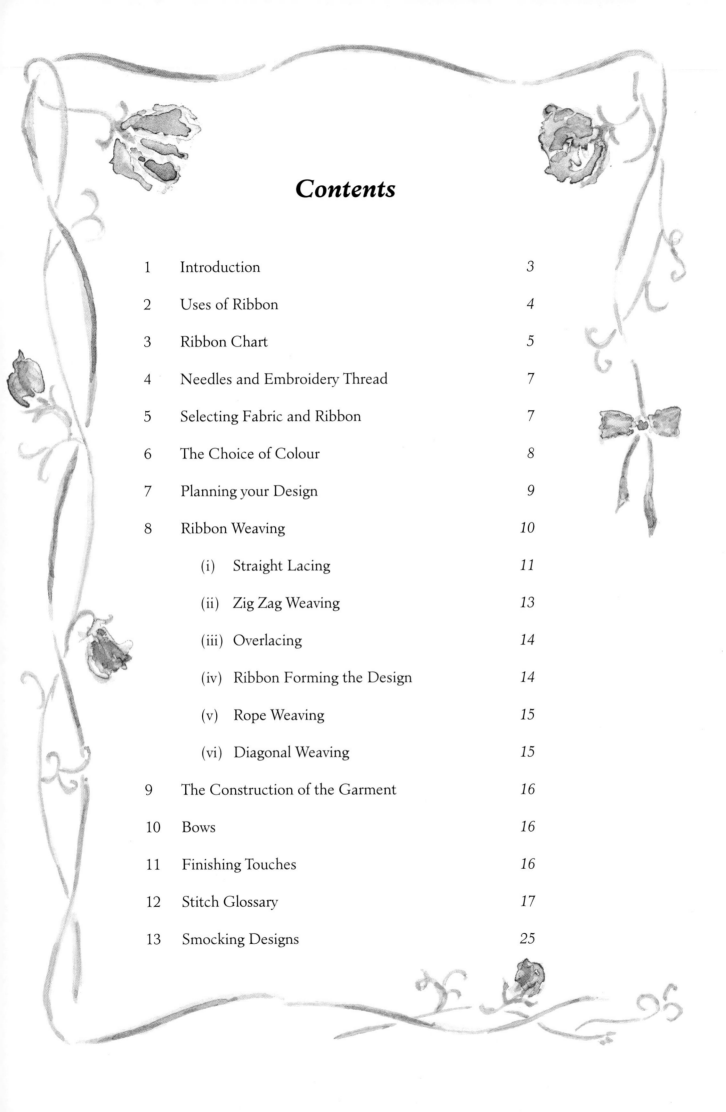

Contents

Acknowledgements

Writing a book is an awesome task which requires the talents of many. I have been greatly blessed, knowing people who willingly help make my dreams come true. My love, appreciation and special thanks go to all those who made this book possible:

To Nicholas Hymns, my creative photographer, who was so patient and dependable, enabling us to capture the perfect photographs.

To all the models who make the pages come alive.

To my darling daughters ... Lynne for the single-finger typing, transcribing my long hand script onto the word processor, and for being my most honest critic. Leigh-Anne, for being so understanding and caring, preparing so many meals for us all.

To my students for their encouragement, enthusiasm and influence spurring me on to do another book and allowing me to use their beautiful garments.

To Debbie Henshilwood for the many hours she spent painstakingly assembling some of the garments for me.

To Susan Koegelenberg for her artistic contributions.

To my special friend, Margie Prestedge, for the time she so generously gave editing this book. Her constructive criticism and constant support are always invaluable.

To Jo Worthington-Smith for her wealth of experience in design and page make-up, and for the many hours spent at her computer developing the unique and excellent graphic illustrations. But especially for her friendship during the long months working together.

A special thank you to my husband, Michael, for all the nights he went to bed alone. Without his encouragement, patience, love and support, I could not have completed this book.

And finally, to Mary Siegel in America, the creator of this technique who sparked my enthusiasm and interest in developing this aspect of smocking.

I feel privileged to have worked with you all.

It is my sincere hope that whether you are a beginner or an experienced smocker, you will be inspired to experiment with ribbon in your designs, creating something unique which gives you great pleasure.

Madeline Bird.

Introduction

T he magic of ribbon will open up a whole new world to enhance your smocking, once you discover the endless variety of texture, contrast and impact created by the use of ribbon. The wonderful colours, sheen, widths and designs will certainly add a new dimension to your smocked garments.

The possibilities are infinite as ribbons are threaded, woven, interlaced or intertwined through the smocked stitches, creating stunning effects.

Ribbon smocking is for all occasions but you can create something quite unique, particularly for that special festive party dress, confirmation or christening gown, with your ribbon smocking.

Gathering ribbons to make frills or ruffles around the neckline, collar or cuffs of a garment adds a touch of femininity, and knitted garments can be further enhanced and individualised by using silk ribbon for surface embroidery.

Various widths of satin ribbon can be used to beautify cushions, curtains, pillows and towels which then compliment any home, not to mention a host of pretty bows that can decorate and personalise that special gift.

Similarly, the spirit of Christmas can be most effectively captured with gaily decorated balls, bells and wreaths, smocked and highlighted with ribbon. A Christmas tree can look exquisite when decorated exclusively with red, green or tartan ribbon.

In fact, no other smocking technique offers so much scope for individual colour co-ordination and interpretation. The inclusion of ribbon in smocking is addictive and it becomes difficult to plan a design without a little touch of ribbon somewhere. Utilising different colours and widths of ribbon within even the simplest design, will transform your smocking into a creative masterpiece.

Uses of Ribbon

Ribbons are available in a wide variety of colours and widths that vary from 1,5 mm to 60 mm. Double faced satin ribbon (which has a satin finish on both sides) is customarily used for weaving through smocking and is particularly recommended for zig zag weaving. Single sided satin ribbon can adequately be used for straight lacing.

The inclusion of ribbon with its endless variety of wonderful colours, widths, sheen and design has the potential to magically transform smocking. By weaving or threading ribbon through the smocked area of a garment, additional impact and textural contrast is achieved. Patterns within patterns evolve as the different widths and colours of ribbon highlight the shades in the fabric – be it patterned, floral or plain.

Silk ribbon is available in 2mm, 4mm and 7mm widths in a wide range of colours and can be used as an alternative to embroidery thread. It adds richness and sheen to designs and is wonderful when used for surface embroidery or to add texture to smocking. Darker shades of silk ribbon may not be colourfast, so careful hand washing of garments in cold water is recommended.

Tartan ribbons are bold and make a statement in both colour and design, to the extent that the ribbon tends to become the dominant feature of a garment. So too with floral, Liberty or designed picture ribbon.

Kinds of ribbon

Double sided satin ribbon

Single sided satin ribbon

Tartan ribbon

Spotted or Dotted ribbon

Designed picture ribbon

Silk ribbon

Floral ribbon (Liberty ribbon)

Taffeta ribbon

Nylon ribbon

Velvet ribbon

Grosgrain ribbon

Gingham ribbon

Fashion Colour Range

Below are just a few samples of ribbon for your guidance.
See your local Berisfords stockist for an enchanting selection of
Ribbon styles, shades and widths.

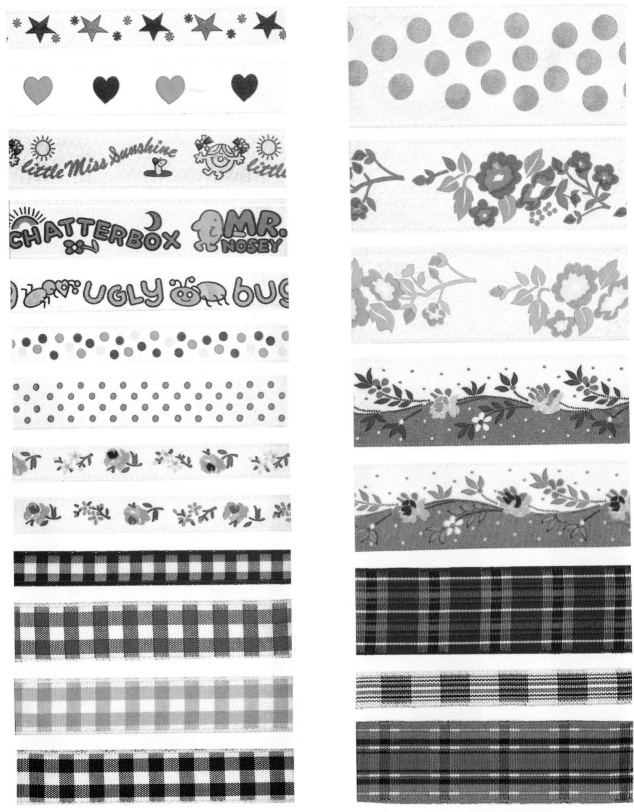

MANUFACTURED BY:
Castellano-Beltrame
Trade Enquiries P O Box 5096, Greenfields, 5208, East London, Republic of South Africa –
Tel: (27) (431) - 312151 – Fax: (27) (431) - 312016

Standard Colour Range

Below are just a few samples of ribbon for your guidance. See your local Berisfords stockist for an enchanting selection of Ribbon styles, shades and widths.

BRIGHT POLYESTER
Sparkle Satin Ribbon

Berisfords

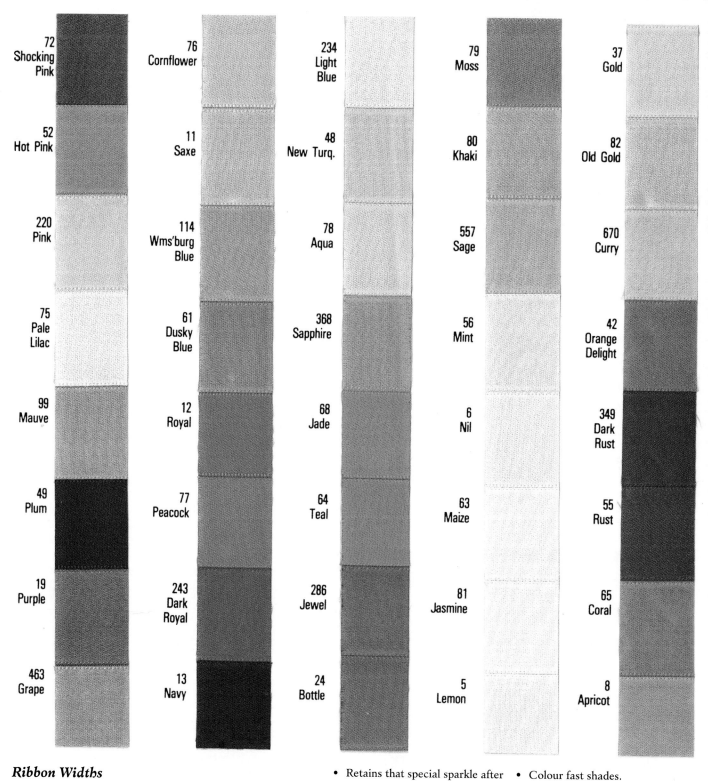

72 Shocking Pink	76 Cornflower	234 Light Blue	79 Moss	37 Gold
52 Hot Pink	11 Saxe	48 New Turq.	80 Khaki	82 Old Gold
220 Pink	114 Wms'burg Blue	78 Aqua	557 Sage	670 Curry
75 Pale Lilac	61 Dusky Blue	368 Sapphire	56 Mint	42 Orange Delight
99 Mauve	12 Royal	68 Jade	6 Nil	349 Dark Rust
49 Plum	77 Peacock	64 Teal	63 Maize	55 Rust
19 Purple	243 Dark Royal	286 Jewel	81 Jasmine	65 Coral
463 Grape	13 Navy	24 Bottle	5 Lemon	8 Apricot

Ribbon Widths

- 3 mm
- 6 mm
- 8 mm
- 10 mm
- 15 mm
- 25 mm
- 38 mm
- 55 mm

- Retains that special sparkle after repeated washing.
- Manufactured from pre-shrunk, stabilized 100% Polyester yarn.
- Unsurpassed quality and versatility.

- Colour fast shades.
- May be dry-cleaned or washed.
- Available in 70 fashionable colours.
- Special colours available on request.

Needles and Embroidery Thread

While a number 7 Crewel needle, which has a sharp point and a long thin eye, is recommended for smocking with embroidery thread, a number 6 Chenille needle, which has a sharp point and a long, broad eye, is preferable for smocking with silk ribbon. This needle will make a big enough hole for the ribbon to pull through the fabric easily. To prevent silk ribbon from fraying use short lengths for embroidery. Tapestry needles, with their blunt points and long, wider eyes, are ideal for ribbon weaving. Straw needles have an extra long shaft and small eye and are recommended for making bullion rosebuds.

Unless otherwise stated, all smocking has been done with Coats Anchor 6 stranded embroidery thread, using four strands on delicate fabrics and six strands on heavier fabrics. Always write down the number of the colour of embroidery thread and ribbon selected. It is always advisable to strip the embroidery thread before using it. Calculate the length of embroidery thread needed for each row by measuring three times the gathered width of the piece to be smocked.

To prevent the end of the silk ribbon from slipping out of the eye of the Chenille needle, insert the point of the needle through the end of the silk ribbon. Thread the other end through the eye of the needle. By pulling the threaded end of the ribbon down the ribbon will be secured at the end.

Selecting Fabric and Ribbon

Fabric choice is very personal and my preference is to smock on natural fibres. An exciting aspect of planning a garment is selecting the fabric from the vast variety available. Smocking on different types of fabric will always yield pleasing results, provided that the fabric is of a good quality. To this end, a wide variety of colours, textures and types of fabric have been used in this book. These include Liberty cotton, Batiste, Swiss voile, pure cotton, polyester cotton, brushed cotton and tartan fabrics.

To assist with fabric selection, some useful questions to ponder before purchasing fabric include: For what occasion is the garment to be worn? For whom is the garment being made? What can I afford?

Regardless of the fabric you choose, be it plain or floral, always select colours you enjoy working with. Having selected the fabric, it is essential to buy the ribbon before purchasing the embroidery cottons, as the range of embroidery thread colours far exceeds that of ribbons. Always buy a little extra ribbon to make allowance for bows that so often add the final touch to a garment. Prewashing a piece of ribbon sewn to a square of the fabric to check for colourfastness is always advisable. Take care to select the correct type of ribbon for the project in mind: narrow, dainty ribbons for infant garments and wider ribbons where the garment is intended for an older child. More adventurous smockers may enjoy combining different widths of ribbon in a design.

The Choice of Colour

*L*ike fabric choice, colour too is very personal, and much inspiration can be gleaned from the wonderful colour nature provides. When designing a new smock, surround yourself with a quantity of coloured ribbons and tones of threads that both compliment and contrast the fabric. Play with the three components of the garment: fabric – ribbon – thread. Many interesting combinations will appear and the choice then becomes that of the variation achieving the most pleasing effect.

Floral and tartan ribbons dictate the colours of the embroidery thread that should be used. Effective designs result from using dark ribbon on pale fabric and light ribbon on dark fabric. Experimenting with colour combinations of both the planned ribbon and thread on a small sampler of the same fabric is essential, as ribbon can change tone once threaded under the smocking stitches. This is particularly applicable to the use of greens and yellows.

Using ribbon in smocking provides a wonderful opportunity to be bold, daring and to have fun with all the colours of the rainbow.

The following rule of selecting embroidery cotton and ribbons is of assistance to even the experienced ribbon smocker and will certainly encourage those new to this aspect of smocking to proceed with their first project with confidence.

The Rule of Three:

1)   A plain pastel shade cotton or polyester cotton fabric.

2)   3 different colour ribbons (One metre of each).

   1st Colour – same colour as fabric but a DARKER shade.
   2nd Colour – any CONTRAST colour to compliment fabric.
   3rd Colour – any CONTRAST colour to compliment fabric.

3)   3 cottons (Embroidery threads to match ribbons).

   1 skein of each:
   1st Colour – same colour as 1st Colour Ribbon.
   2nd Colour – same colour as 2nd Colour Ribbon.
   3rd Colour – same colour as 3rd Colour Ribbon.

When planning your design always try to have all three colour components in each section of the design. Careful study of designs *Susan* (page 49), *Leanne* (page 56), *Nicola* (page 66) and *Cushions to dream on* (page 93), are good examples of the "Rule of Three" in practice.

Planning your Design

Simple, traditional patterns can be recreated by incorporating ribbon, thereby changing an old favorite design into a special and unique creation. The ribbons become the dominant feature of the design rather than the smocking stitches as they form their own designs within the smocking pattern. The versatile Chevron stitch with all its combinations is the stitch of preference for ribbon weaving. However, stitch length is critical and is dependent on the width of the ribbon that is being used. It may be necessary to smock above or below the gathering rows in order to facilitate the width of ribbon to be used. Halfspace stitching is used for thin dainty ribbon, while bigger stitches are needed for bolder designs that require thicker ribbon. Always check that the ribbon weaves through the stitches easily, by working a sampler before you begin.

Designs don't have to be complicated to be effective. Simple stitch combinations best lend themselves to ribbon smocking as they are often covered by the ribbon and the emphasis becomes concentrated entirely on the ribbons and on colour. For more intricate patterns, ribbons and embroidery cottons need to be mixed and blended to achieve the correct balance and desired effect.

When smocking on tartan fabric, the gathering threads act only as guidelines to help keep the design straight. Smock on the horizontal tartan lines.

As the ribbon is the major feature of the smocking, it is essential to centre both the smocking design and the ribbon so that both begin and end in exactly the same way on the first and last pleat of any smocked piece. It is important that the design is symmetrical from side to side.

Work out the design before pleating the fabric. Fold the fabric in half and mark the centre by tacking down the length of the fabric with a contrast thread. Work out the design repeat and start the first row of the motif on the two centre pleats, working towards the right hand side of the pleated piece. Turn the work upside down and, once again starting at the centre, work the opposite side of the first row. Each successive row of smocking must begin and end on the same pleat. Leave only 3 pleats free of smocking on either side of the smocked piece so that the ends of the ribbon, once woven through the smocking, can be caught in the side seams. Ribbon ended this way tends to wear better once the garment has been washed.

Accent stitches in the form of Bullion rosebuds, French Knots and surface embroidery add special finishing touches to smocking.

Ribbon Weaving

Ribbons can be threaded through smocking horizontally, vertically or diagonally. Another variation is to thread ribbon from either side to the centre of the smocking, finishing it off by tying a bow. This method is particularly effective for circular neck garments. Ribbon is woven through the smocking, using a blunt ended Tapestry needle, after the gathering threads have been removed and the pieces blocked to fit the yoke. Take care not to pull the embroidery threads when weaving under the stitches. Cut the ends of the ribbon diagonally to facilitate the threading of the needle. Once the ribbon is threaded through the Tapestry needle, fold the end over and catch it down with a few stitches. This will prevent the needle from constantly falling off the ribbon as you thread it through the smocking.

When superimposing one ribbon on top of another, use tissue paper between the two ribbons as you stitch, to stop the top ribbon from slipping. After stitching, tear away the tissue paper. Although the quoted ribbon meterage is generous, it can only be approximate, as much depends on the size of the garment. To prevent the ends of bows from fraying, seal them with "Fray Check", clear nail varnish or run the ends through a flame.

An alternative use of wider ribbon is to stitch it by machine to the smocking once blocking is completed. This is done by stitching along two rows of back smocking. As ribbon does not stretch, the elasticity of the smocked area is reduced by the use of straight lacing. It is therefore advisable not to finish off the ends of the ribbon or to machine stitch wider ribbon to the smocking until the garment is at a stage where it can be fitted on the child.

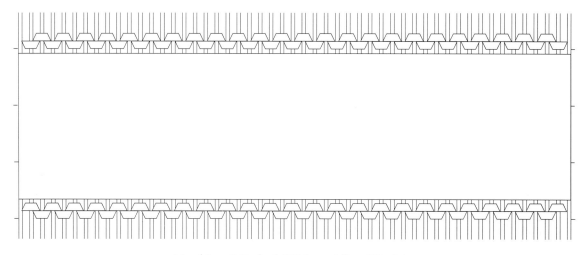

Machine Stitched Ribbon After Blocking

Similarly, wider ribbon may be sewn by machine to the section of fabric to be pleated. The fabric is then put through the pleater, care being taken to align the ribbon with the gathering rows. This method is splendidly shown on the *Chiara* design (page 82).

Straight Lacing

For a straight lacing, any width of single sided satin ribbon can be threaded through the smocking from one side to the other. The ribbon is threaded under each stitch. The width of the ribbon may sometimes make it necessary to vertically lengthen the stitches.

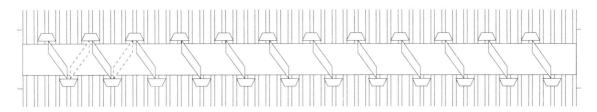

Halfspace Half Chevron

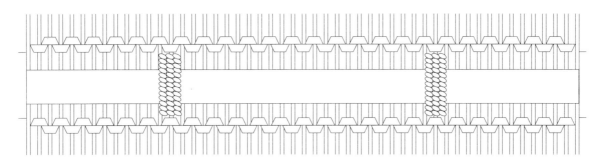

Vertical Bullion Rosebuds

Ribbon is threaded under vertical bullion rosebuds. These are anchored at the top and bottom points on cable stitches. Using 3 strands of embroidery cotton do 15 wraps per winding.

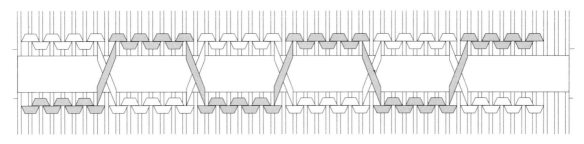

Crossed Lacing

Careful forethought and planning are vital keys when planning a design which requires the ribbon to be threaded through vertical buttonholes in the smocking. Make a sample buttonhole on a scrap of fabric and check that the buttonhole will adequately allow the ribbon to pass through it without distorting it. Pleat a sample piece of fabric in order to calculate the number of pleats required between each buttonhole.

Before pleating the piece to be smocked, thread the needles of the pleater with gathering threads that are the same length as the width of fabric. This will enable the pleats to be pulled out and the fabric smoothed flat, so that the positions of the buttonholes can be marked and made in the valleys. Once this is done, pull up gathering threads again and proceed with the smocking. After completing the design, remove the gathering threads and only then cut the buttonholes open. Weave the ribbon in and out of the buttonholes. Backsmock any areas that "bubble".

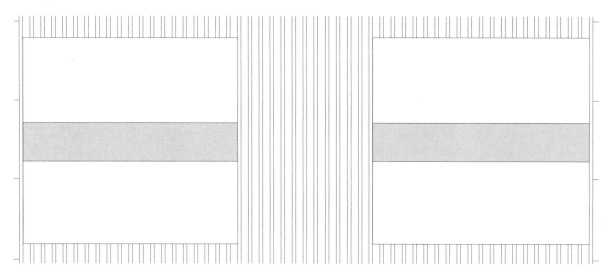

Vertical Buttonholes

It is important to bear in mind that the finished garment will lose its elasticity when using straight lacing, so it may be necessary to allow extra width before pleating the fabric. As a general rule of thumb, cotton fabrics will be reduced to a third of their original width when smocked, while Batiste and voile will be reduced to a quarter of their original width.

Zig Zag Weaving

For zig zag weaving the most pleasing effect is achieved by using double sided 1.5 mm or 3 mm satin ribbon. The variations of zig zag weaving are almost limitless and each lacing requires ribbon approximately three times the length of the row.

Zig zag lacings have ribbon woven under each stitch. Thread a tapestry needle with the required length of ribbon. Pull approximately half this length of ribbon through the centre chevron stitch of the design, leaving the other half free. Weave the ribbon from the centre of the design to the right hand side of the piece. Turn the work upside down and starting at the centre again, weave the ribbon to the left hand side of the piece. At the top and bottom points of the zig zag, fold the ribbon into the correct position and hold it under your thumb. Thread it under the first chevron of the new direction and check that the ribbon is folded correctly. Continue to thread it through the remainder of the stitches, picking up as many stitches as possible on the needle before pulling the ribbon through. Straighten the ribbon before pulling it through the stitches. Take care not to stretch the stitches or split the cotton. To secure the ribbon, machine stitch it into the side seams or turn the ends back on themselves and stitch them neatly to the smocking.

Weaving Under Each Stitch

Weaving Under and Over Each Stitch

Over-under lacing is done through a row of chevron diamonds. The ribbon is alternated under and over the adjacent chevron stitch after changing direction.

Overlacing

Lacing over previously laced ribbon is very effective and lends itself to endless experimentation. Having completed the first ribbon weaving, select another colour or width of ribbon and weave a second design over the first.

Overlacing Under Each Stitch

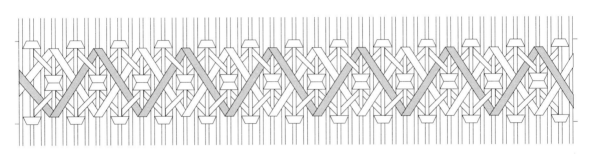

Overlacing Under and Over Each Stitch

Ribbon Forming the Design

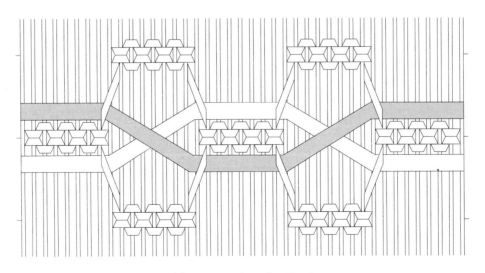

Ribbon Forming the Design

Rope Weaving

Rope weaving is done through half space chevrons. Thread the ribbon from right to left over and then under the second chevron stitch. Pulling the ribbon taught, skip the adjacent chevron and then go over and under the next chevron, once again going from left to right. Continue across the row in this way. This method is particularly effective as a border for the top and bottom of a design. It has no stretch at all, however, and must be done only when the garment is constructed to the stage when it can be fitted on the child.

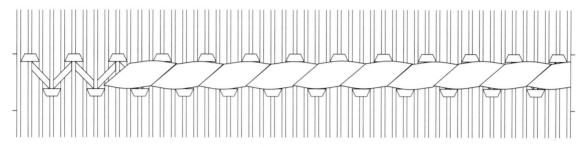

Rope Weaving

Diagonal Weaving

Work several rows of chevron diamonds one below the other. Remove gathering thread rows and block the smocked piece to the finished width. Starting at the bottom of the centre front, pull half the length of ribbon through the centre chevron stitch. Weave the ribbon diagonally up the right side of the design under each stitch to the shoulder seam. Repeat this process on the left side. Experiment by weaving many interesting patterns through a lattice design.

Diagonal Weaving

The Construction of the Garment

*A*fter removing gathering threads, block the smocking by pinning it to an ironing board. Hold a hot steam iron just above the smocked piece, taking care not to touch the smocking with the iron. Once this step is completed, lace the ribbon through the smocking and attach it to the yoke. To prevent the ribbon from slipping, tack it down on either side of the underarm shaping, before cutting out the armhole. Adjust the ribbon in the straight or zig zag weaving to prevent the ribbon distorting, before stitching the side seams.

Ribbon smocking on a child's sleeves is very practical as well as adding to the garment's appealing appearance. This is done by threading ribbon through a row of chevrons on the lower edge of the sleeve. Untie the bows on the sleeves to facilitate dressing and undressing. The same applies around the ankle of a smocked babygro.

For a professional finish to garments, always press with a steam iron. It is preferable to hand wash garments incorporating ribbon.

Bows

*B*ows play a tremendous part in the finished appearance of your design. On a straight lacing, thread ribbon from one side of the smocking to the other and sew a separate bow on afterwards, where desired. On a bishop neck garment, lace the ribbon from the centre back to the front on either side and tie the bow at the centre front and stitch it into place.

Finishing Touches

*W*hen planning the construction of your creative masterpiece, spend time on the finishing touches to collars, sleeves and hems. Cuffs and collars can be added in a contrasting fabric to compliment the garment. Similarly, using piping on collars and sleeves is an effective way of introducing a contrast colour to match the smocking and ribbon, achieving colour balance and maximum visual impact.

Feminine frills at the neck and on the sleeves give the garment a festive finish, while at the hemline of a child's dress a ruffle or ribbon sewn between tucks adds extra charm.

For those special garments, use fancy collars or exquisite lace to create an heirloom for future generations to enjoy.

Stitch Glossary

1 Stem Stitch and Outline Stitch

2 Cable Stitch

3 Chevron

4 Halfspace Chevron

5 Cable and Chevron

6 Cable and Chevron

7 Trellis

8 Cable and Trellis

9 Cable and Trellis

10 Rosebud

1 Stem Stitch and Outline Stitch

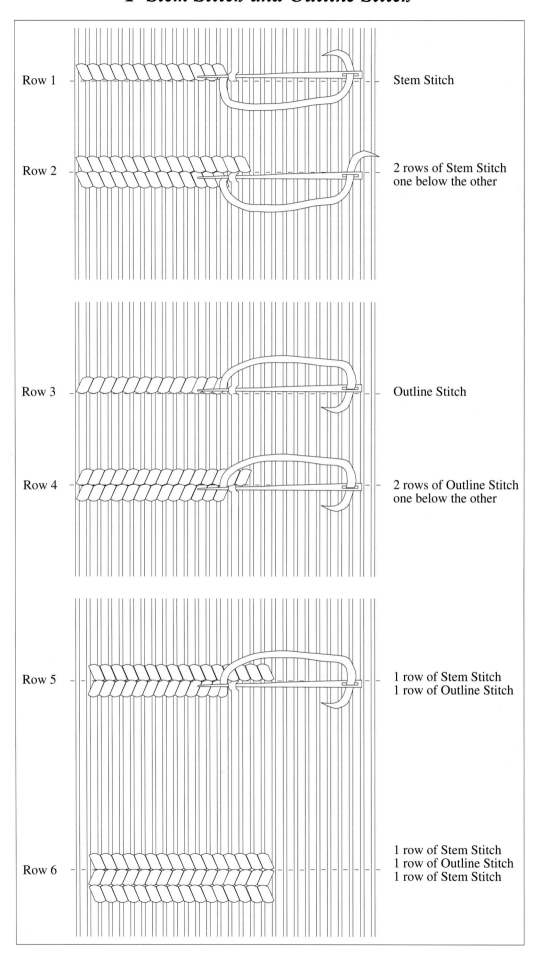

Row 1 — Stem Stitch

Row 2 — 2 rows of Stem Stitch one below the other

Row 3 — Outline Stitch

Row 4 — 2 rows of Outline Stitch one below the other

Row 5 — 1 row of Stem Stitch 1 row of Outline Stitch

Row 6 — 1 row of Stem Stitch 1 row of Outline Stitch 1 row of Stem Stitch

2 Cable Stitch

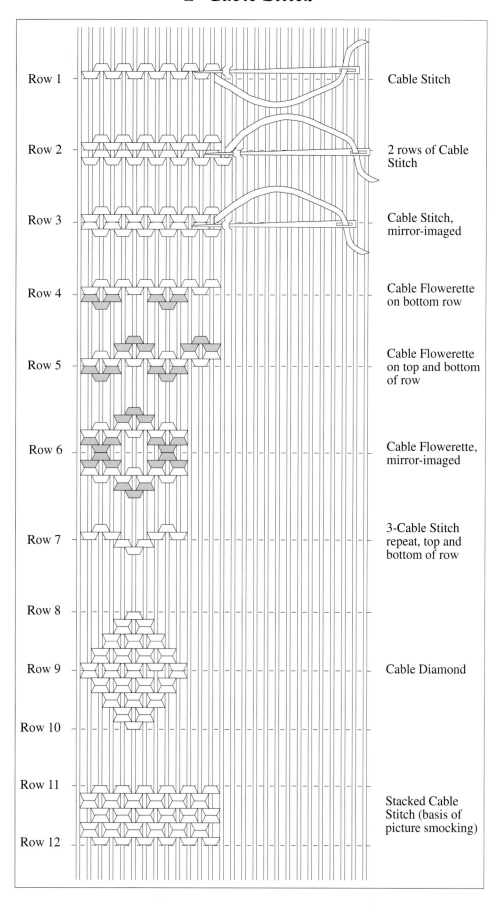

Row 1 — Cable Stitch

Row 2 — 2 rows of Cable Stitch

Row 3 — Cable Stitch, mirror-imaged

Row 4 — Cable Flowerette on bottom row

Row 5 — Cable Flowerette on top and bottom of row

Row 6 — Cable Flowerette, mirror-imaged

Row 7 — 3-Cable Stitch repeat, top and bottom of row

Row 8

Row 9 — Cable Diamond

Row 10

Row 11 — Stacked Cable Stitch (basis of picture smocking)

Row 12

3 Chevron

Row 1

Row 2 — Chevron

Row 3

Row 4 — Chevron, mirror-imaged

Row 5

Row 6 — Chevron Diamond

Row 7

Row 8 — Chevron Crossed

Row 9

Row 10 — Chevron with halfspace Chevron crossed at bottom

Row 11

Row 12 — Chevron with halfspace Chevron crossed at top

Row 13

4 Halfspace Chevron

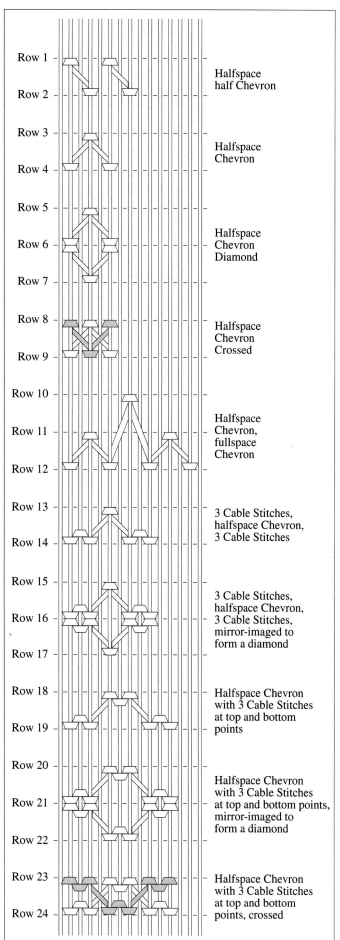

Row 1

Row 2 — Halfspace half Chevron

Row 3

Row 4 — Halfspace Chevron

Row 5

Row 6 — Halfspace Chevron Diamond

Row 7

Row 8 — Halfspace Chevron Crossed

Row 9

Row 10

Row 11 — Halfspace Chevron, fullspace Chevron

Row 12

Row 13 — 3 Cable Stitches, halfspace Chevron, 3 Cable Stitches

Row 14

Row 15 — 3 Cable Stitches, halfspace Chevron, 3 Cable Stitches, mirror-imaged to form a diamond

Row 16

Row 17

Row 18 — Halfspace Chevron with 3 Cable Stitches at top and bottom points

Row 19

Row 20 — Halfspace Chevron with 3 Cable Stitches at top and bottom points, mirror-imaged to form a diamond

Row 21

Row 22

Row 23 — Halfspace Chevron with 3 Cable Stitches at top and bottom points, crossed

Row 24

5 Cable and Chevron

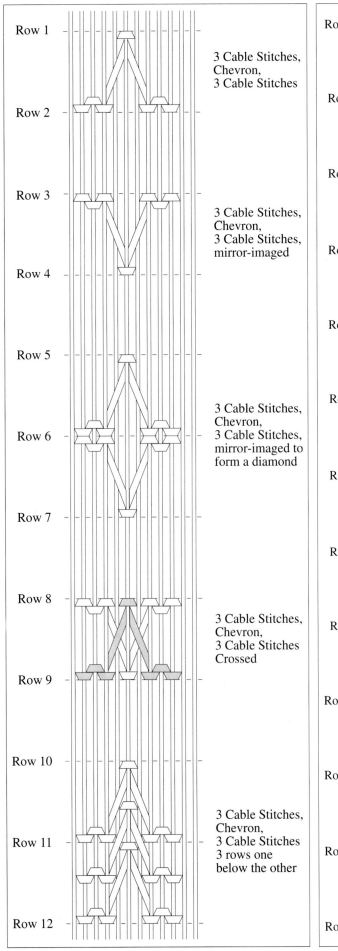

Row 1

3 Cable Stitches,
Chevron,
3 Cable Stitches

Row 2

Row 3

3 Cable Stitches,
Chevron,
3 Cable Stitches,
mirror-imaged

Row 4

Row 5

Row 6

3 Cable Stitches,
Chevron,
3 Cable Stitches,
mirror-imaged to
form a diamond

Row 7

Row 8

3 Cable Stitches,
Chevron,
3 Cable Stitches
Crossed

Row 9

Row 10

Row 11

3 Cable Stitches,
Chevron,
3 Cable Stitches
3 rows one
below the other

Row 12

6 Cable and Chevron

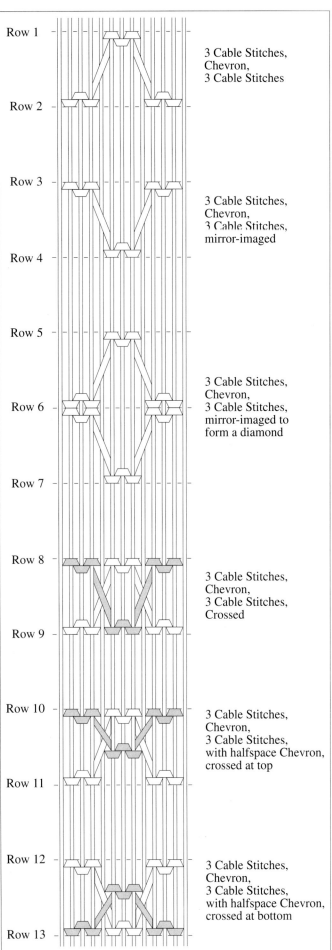

Row 1

3 Cable Stitches,
Chevron,
3 Cable Stitches

Row 2

Row 3

3 Cable Stitches,
Chevron,
3 Cable Stitches,
mirror-imaged

Row 4

Row 5

Row 6

3 Cable Stitches,
Chevron,
3 Cable Stitches,
mirror-imaged to
form a diamond

Row 7

Row 8

3 Cable Stitches,
Chevron,
3 Cable Stitches,
Crossed

Row 9

Row 10

3 Cable Stitches,
Chevron,
3 Cable Stitches,
with halfspace Chevron,
crossed at top

Row 11

Row 12

3 Cable Stitches,
Chevron,
3 Cable Stitches,
with halfspace Chevron,
crossed at bottom

Row 13

7 *Trellis*

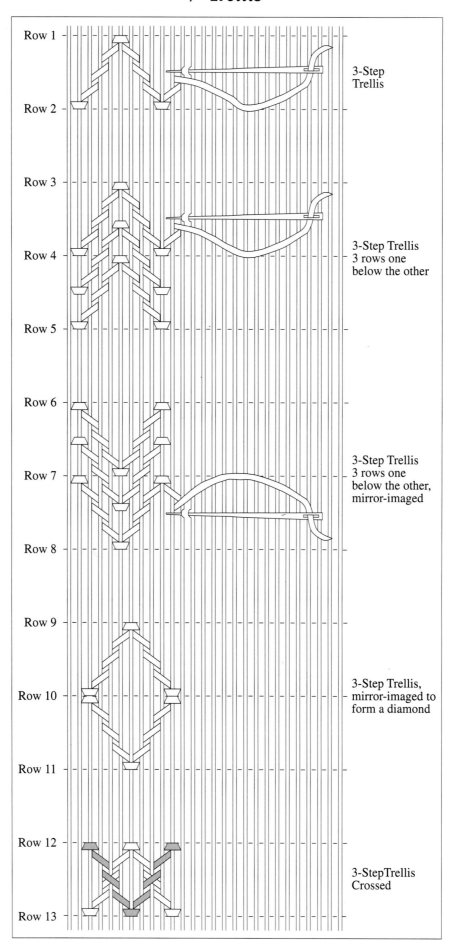

Row 1

Row 2

3-Step
Trellis

Row 3

Row 4

3-Step Trellis
3 rows one
below the other

Row 5

Row 6

Row 7

3-Step Trellis
3 rows one
below the other,
mirror-imaged

Row 8

Row 9

Row 10

3-Step Trellis,
mirror-imaged to
form a diamond

Row 11

Row 12

3-StepTrellis
Crossed

Row 13

8 Cable and Trellis

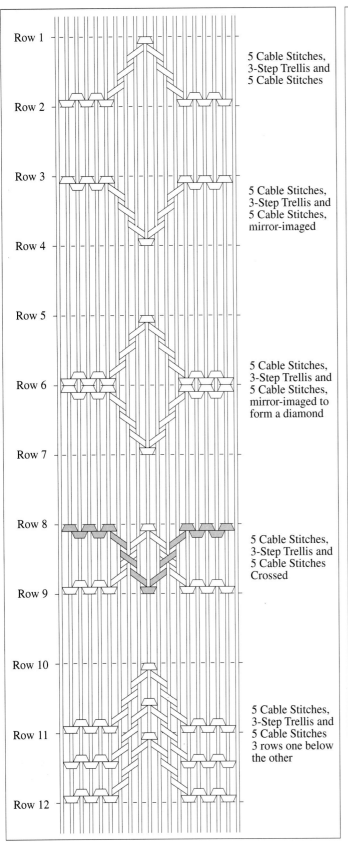

Row 1

Row 2 — 5 Cable Stitches, 3-Step Trellis and 5 Cable Stitches

Row 3

Row 4 — 5 Cable Stitches, 3-Step Trellis and 5 Cable Stitches, mirror-imaged

Row 5

Row 6 — 5 Cable Stitches, 3-Step Trellis and 5 Cable Stitches, mirror-imaged to form a diamond

Row 7

Row 8 — 5 Cable Stitches, 3-Step Trellis and 5 Cable Stitches Crossed

Row 9

Row 10

Row 11 — 5 Cable Stitches, 3-Step Trellis and 5 Cable Stitches 3 rows one below the other

Row 12

9 Cable and Trellis

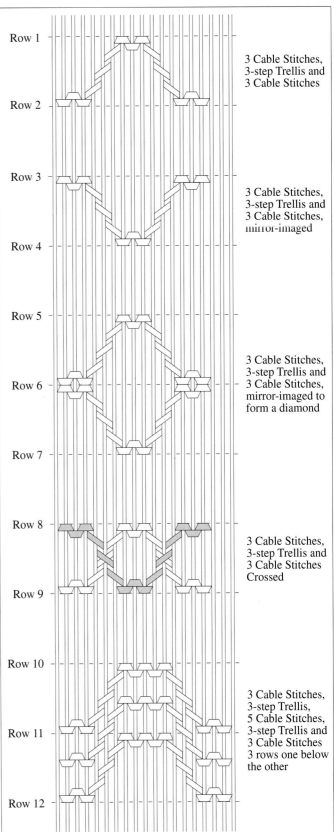

Row 1

Row 2 — 3 Cable Stitches, 3-step Trellis and 3 Cable Stitches

Row 3

Row 4 — 3 Cable Stitches, 3-step Trellis and 3 Cable Stitches, mirror-imaged

Row 5

Row 6 — 3 Cable Stitches, 3-step Trellis and 3 Cable Stitches, mirror-imaged to form a diamond

Row 7

Row 8 — 3 Cable Stitches, 3-step Trellis and 3 Cable Stitches Crossed

Row 9

Row 10

Row 11 — 3 Cable Stitches, 3-step Trellis, 5 Cable Stitches, 3-step Trellis and 3 Cable Stitches 3 rows one below the other

Row 12

23

10 Rosebud

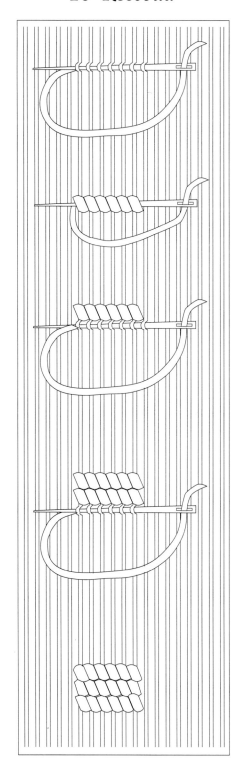

Smocking Designs

Frieda

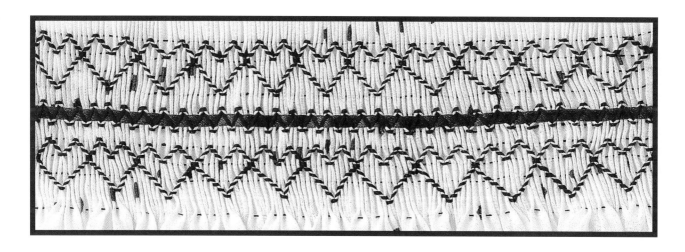

Smocked on halfspace smocking rows.
Thread pleater with 12 halfspace rows of
cotton and pleat fabric.
Do not smock on rows 1 and 12.
Always centre the design.

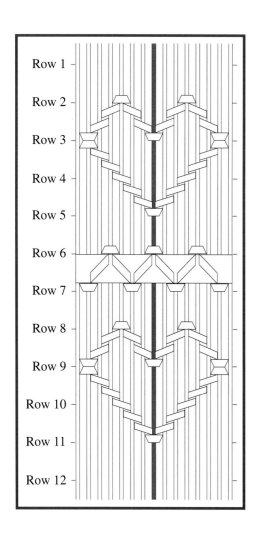

Row 1
Row 2
Row 3
Row 4
Row 5
Row 6
Row 7
Row 8
Row 9
Row 10
Row 11
Row 12

Ribbon Design

• Weave 3 mm satin ribbon under the halfspace chevrons.

Coats Anchor Stranded Cotton		
No 046	Red	
Berisford Ribbon		
No 15	Red	3 mm
Ribbon Lengths Required		
x 25 cm	Dress	x 10 "
x 80 cm	Sleeves	x 32 "

Caitlin

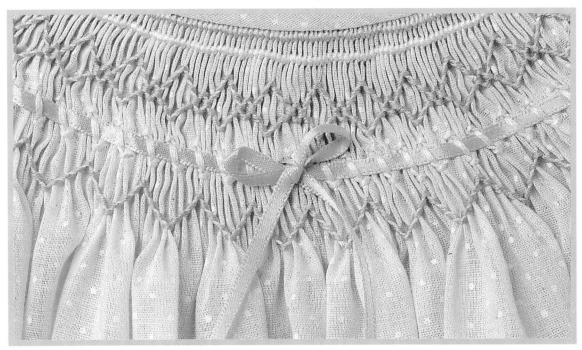

**Smocked on halfspace smocking rows.
Thread pleater with 14 halfspace rows of cotton
and pleat fabric.
Do not smock on rows 1, 2, 13 and 14.
Always centre the design.**

Ribbon Design

- Weave 3 mm satin ribbon under halfspace chevrons.

Coats Anchor Stranded Cotton

No 0203	Green	
No 0292	Yellow	
No 050	Pink	

Berisford Ribbon

No 56	Mint Green	3mm

Ribbon Length Required

x 1.30 metres	Mint Green	x 51 "

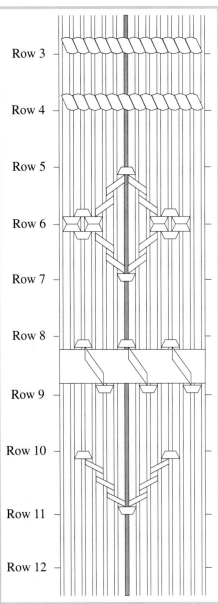

Row 3

Row 4

Row 5

Row 6

Row 7

Row 8

Row 9

Row 10

Row 11

Row 12

Vanessa

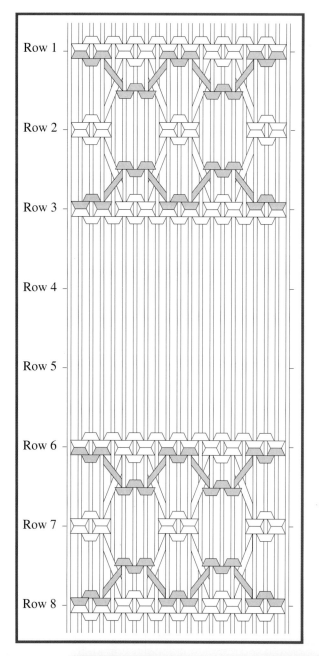

Row 1
Row 2
Row 3
Row 4
Row 5
Row 6
Row 7
Row 8

**Thread pleater with 23 rows of cotton
and pleat fabric.
Do not smock on rows 1 and 23.
Always centre the design.**

Design

- Leave 6 flutes unsmocked in the centre of the fabric for the bows.
- Smocking is done on the lines of the tartan design. When smocking on tartan fabric, the gathering threads act as guidelines, and help keep the design straight.
- Backsmock in cable between rows 4 and 5, 9 and 10, 14 and 15, and 19 and 20, using 2 strands of embroidery cotton.
- Decorative bows are stitched down the centre of the design.
- Ribbon and lace are stitched to the belt.

Coats Anchor Stranded Cotton
No 020   Scarlet

Berisford Ribbon
No 908   Scarlet Berry   25 mm
No 908   Scarlet Berry   3 mm

Ribbon Lengths Required
x 1.5 metres   Belt   x 59 "
x 1.5 metres   Bows   x 59 "

Lauren

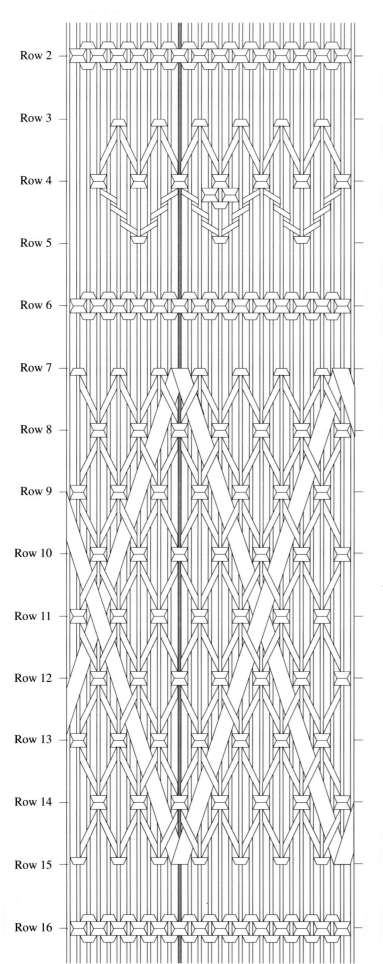

Row 2
Row 3
Row 4
Row 5
Row 6
Row 7
Row 8
Row 9
Row 10
Row 11
Row 12
Row 13
Row 14
Row 15
Row 16

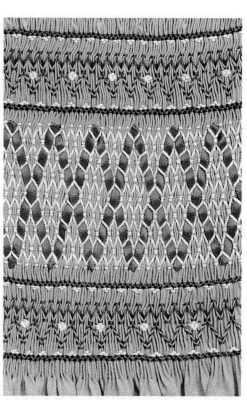

Thread pleater with 21 rows of cotton and pleat fabric.
Do not smock on rows 1 and 21.
Always centre the design.

Ribbon Design

- Cut the ribbon into two lengths. Fold each length in half.
- Start weaving at centre top apex of the chevron design, according to the diagram.
- See *Zig Zag Weaving*, page 13.
- Mirror-image from row 11 to row 20 to complete the design.

Coats Anchor Stranded Cotton
No 0292   Yellow
No 0133   Blue

Berisford Ribbon
No 243   Dark Royal   3 mm

Ribbon Length Required
Double-sided satin ribbon
x 5 metres   Dark Royal   x 197 "

Nicky

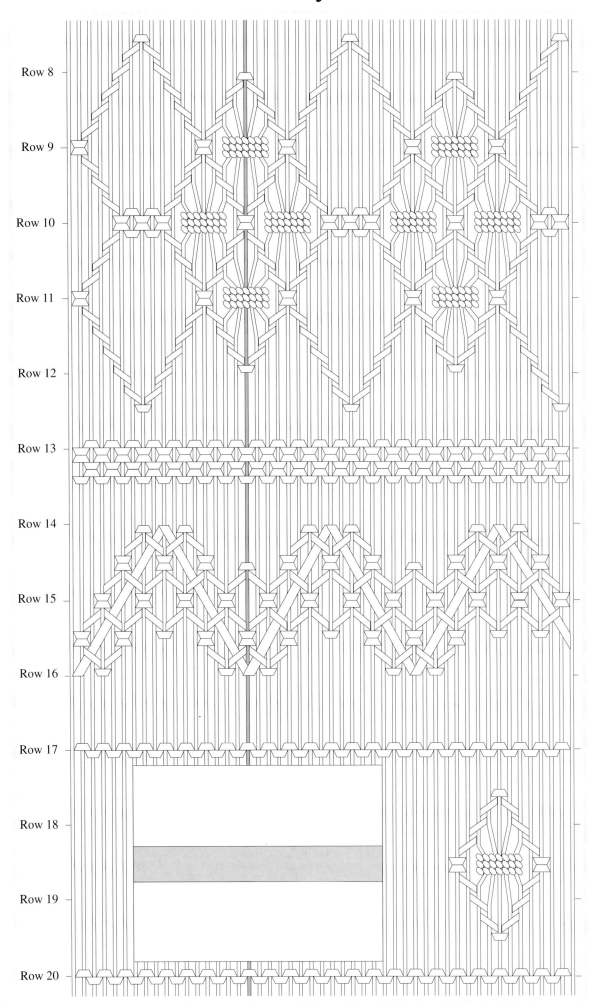

Row 8

Row 9

Row 10

Row 11

Row 12

Row 13

Row 14

Row 15

Row 16

Row 17

Row 18

Row 19

Row 20

Nicky

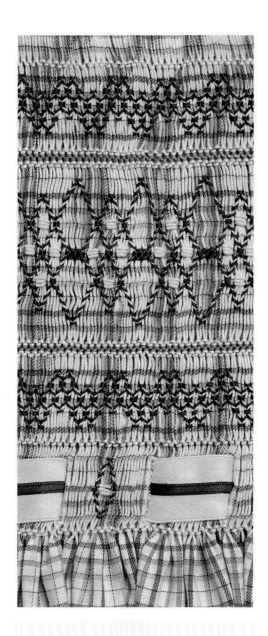

**Thread pleater with 21 rows of cotton
and pleat fabric.
Do not smock on rows 1 and 21.
Always centre the design.**

Ribbon Design

- Ribbon is woven between rows 17 and 20.
- Skip 5 pleats and mark the valley of the next pleat with a vertical tacking thread.
- Working across, count 23 pleats from the first tacking thread and mark the next valley. Continue across leaving 5 pleats at the end of the row.
- Make 2.5 cm vertical buttonholes in the valleys.
- Backsmock between the buttonholes on rows 19 and 20.
- In the centred area, where the ribbon passes behind, work a 3-step diamond design.
- Weave 25 mm satin ribbon through the buttonholes.
- To achieve extra colour, stitch 3 mm ribbon onto the centre of the wider ribbon.
- See *Straight Lacing*, page 12.

Coats Anchor Stranded Cotton

No 0292	Yellow	
No 0132	Blue	

Berisford Ribbon

No 5	Lemon	25 mm
No 5	Lemon	3 mm
No 243	Dark Royal	3 mm

Ribbon Lengths Required

x 2 metres	Lemon	x 80 "
x 2 metres	Lemon	x 80 "
x 2 metres	Dark Royal	x 80 "

Alexandra

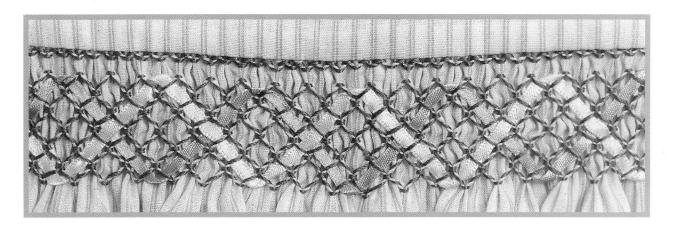

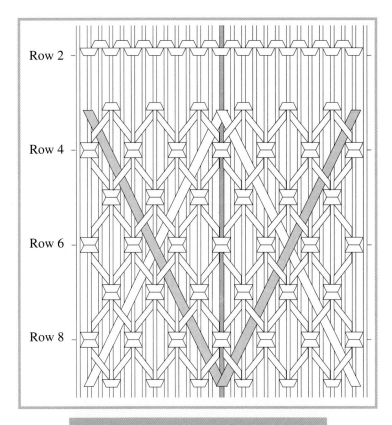

Smocked on halfspace
smocking rows.
Thread pleater with 10 halfspace rows
of cotton and pleat fabric.
Do not smock on rows 1 and 10.
Always centre the design.

Ribbon Design

- Start weaving at the centre top apex of the chevron design, according to the diagram.
- See *Overlacing*, page 14.

Coats Anchor Stranded Cotton

No 052	Pink	

Berisford Ribbon

No 220	Pink	3 mm
No 1	White	3 mm

Ribbon Lengths Required

x 35 cm	Pink	x 14 "
x 35 cm	White	x 14 "

Tamsin

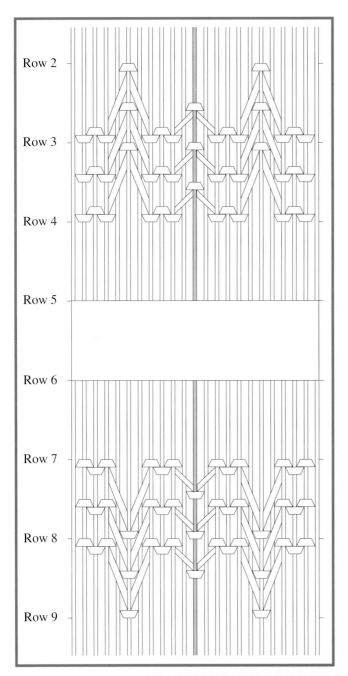

Row 2

Row 3

Row 4

Row 5

Row 6

Row 7

Row 8

Row 9

**Thread pleater with 10 rows of cotton
and pleat fabric.
Do not smock on rows 1 and 10.
Always centre the design.**

Ribbon Design

- Stitch ribbon to fabric between rows 5 and 6.
- See *Ribbon Weaving*, page 10.

Coats Anchor Stranded Cotton		
No 0133	Blue	
No 0243	Green	
No 0295	Yellow	
Berisford Ribbon		
Printed Ribbon		15 mm
Ribbon Lengths Required		
x 50 cm	Printed Ribbon	x 20 "

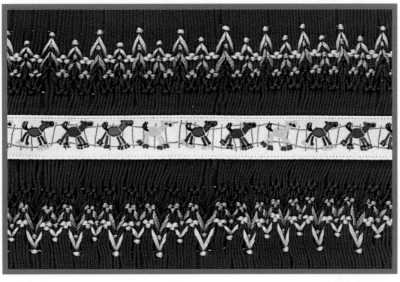

Justine

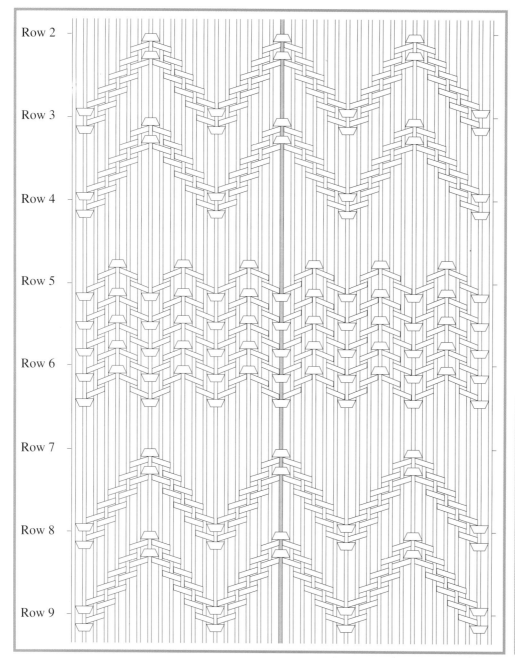

Row 2

Row 3

Row 4

Row 5

Row 6

Row 7

Row 8

Row 9

Thread pleater with 10 rows of cotton and pleat fabric.
Do not smock on rows 1 and 10.
Always centre the design.

Ribbon Design

- Ribbon is used for bows and above hemline frill.

Coats Anchor Stranded Cotton

No 052	Pink
No 049	Pink

Berisford Ribbon

No 60	Dusky Pink 3 mm

Ribbon Lengths Required

x 1 metre	Dusky
x 40 "	Pink

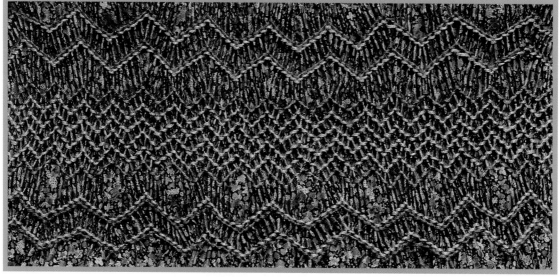

Smocked by Barbara Dowling

Susan

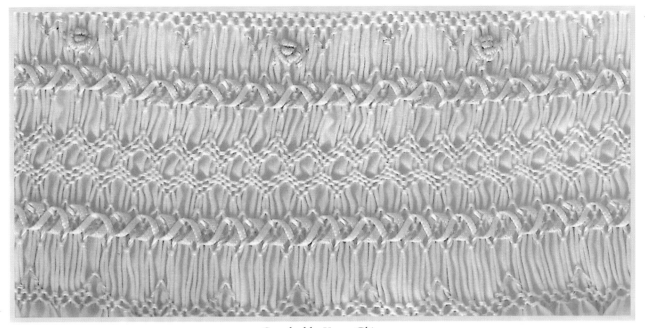

Smocked by Verna Chinn

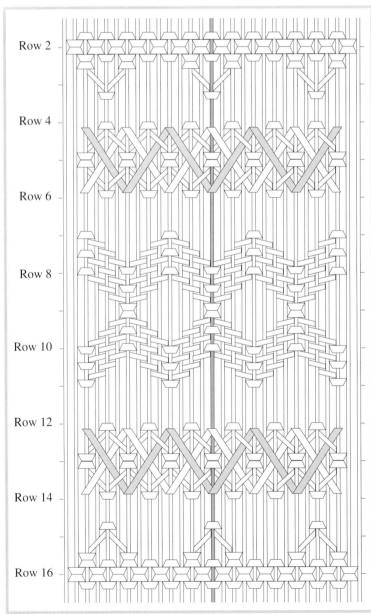

**Smocked on halfspace
smocking rows.
Thread pleater with 17 halfspace
rows of cotton and pleat fabric.
Do not smock on rows 1 and 17.
Always centre the design.**

Ribbon Design

- Weave ribbon according to the diagram.
- See *Overlacing*, page 14.

Coats Anchor Stranded Cotton

No 048	Pink	
No 0214	Green	
No 0926	Cream	

Berisford Ribbon

No 70	Pale Pink	1.5 mm
No 56	Mint	1.5 mm

Ribbon Lengths Required

x 1 metre	Pink	Dress	x 40 "
x 1 metre	Mint	Sleeves	x 40 "
x 2.25 metres		Skirt	x 88 "

43

Kristy

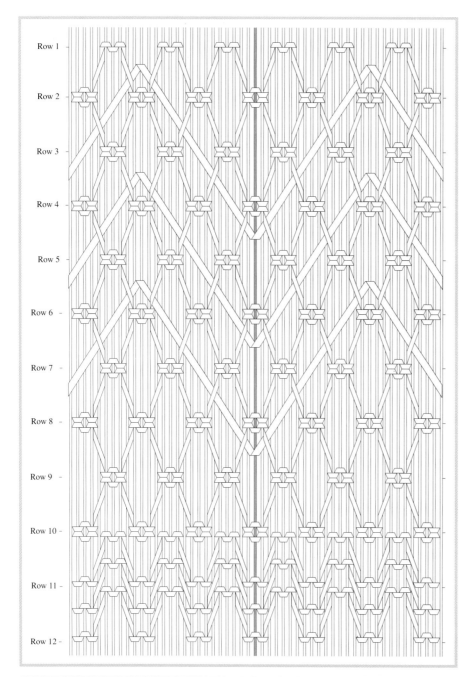

Row 1
Row 2
Row 3
Row 4
Row 5
Row 6
Row 7
Row 8
Row 9
Row 10
Row 11
Row 12

**Thread pleater with
14 rows of cotton and
pleat fabric.
Do not smock on row 13.
Always centre the design.**

Ribbon Design

- Start weaving at the centre of the chevron design according to the diagram.
- See *Diagonal Weaving*, page 15.

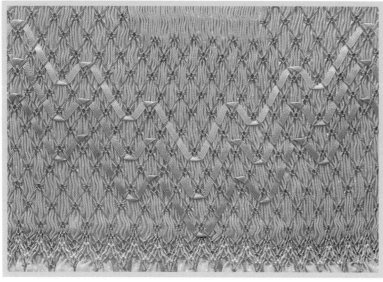

Coats Anchor Stranded Cotton

No 049	Pink	
No 0203	Green	
No 01	White	

Berisford Ribbon

No 1	White	3 mm
No 220	Pink	3 mm
No 56	Mint	3 mm

Ribbon Lengths Required
Double sided satin ribbon
x 50 cm   White, Pink & Mint   x 20 "

Leanne

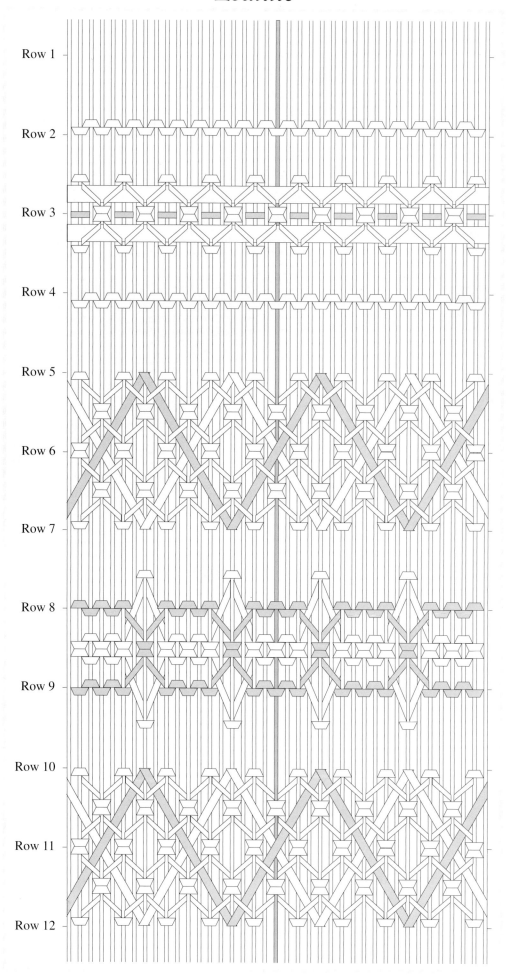

Row 1

Row 2

Row 3

Row 4

Row 5

Row 6

Row 7

Row 8

Row 9

Row 10

Row 11

Row 12

Leanne

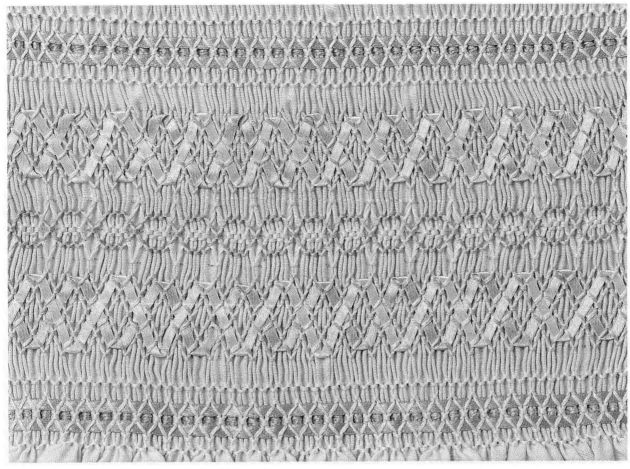

Smocked by Lynette Botha

**Thread pleater with 17 rows of cotton
and pleat fabric.
Do not smock on rows 1 and 17.
Always centre the design.
See *Rule of Three*, page 8.**

Ribbon Design

- See *Straight Lacing*, page 11, and *Overlacing*, page 14.
- Weave ribbon according to the diagram.
- Mirror-image design from row 9 to row 16.

Coats Anchor Stranded Cotton

No 0386	Yellow	
No 050	Pink	
No 0159	Blue	

Berisford Ribbon

No 63	Maize	3 mm
No 2	Pink	3 mm
No 76	Cornflower	3 mm

Ribbon Lengths Required

x 1.25 metres	Maize	x 49 "
x 1.25 metres	Pink	x 49 "
x 1.25 metres	Cornflower	x 49 "

**Photograph on pages 46 and 47, from left to right:
Nicola's dress smocked by Penny Trevett;
Carrie and Sue-Anne's dresses smocked by Sharon Venn;
Leanne's dress smocked by Lynette Botha.**

Lerí

Embroidery by Susan Koegelenberg

**Thread pleater with 32 rows of cotton and pleat fabric.
Do not smock on rows 2 and 32.
Always centre the design.**

- Draw the heart design in the centre of the smocking with a water soluble pen or tailor's chalk.
- Embroidery stitches worked using 3 strands of cotton.

Ribbon Design

- Ribbon is stitched to form a 'V' after gathering threads have been removed.

Coats Anchor Stranded Cotton	
No 0109	Mauve
No 0131	Blue
No 0108	Lilac
No 0186	Turquoise

Ribbon

Liberty or printed ribbon	25 mm

Ribbon Lengths Required

x 1 metre	Liberty	Dress	x 40 "
x 2.25 metres	Liberty	Skirt	x 88 "

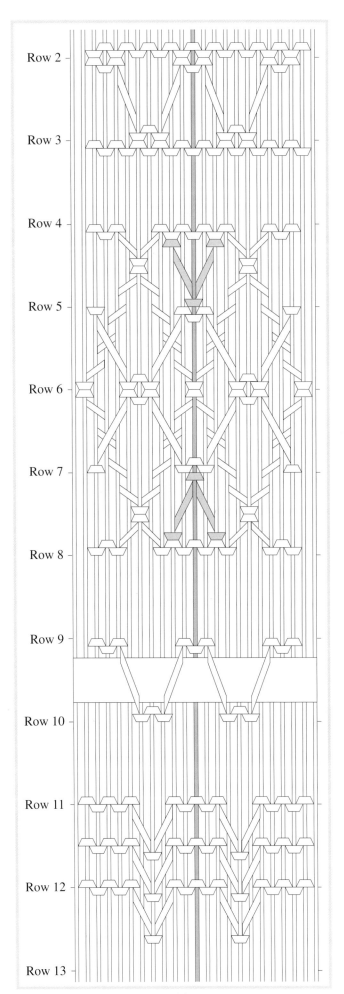

Row 2
Row 3
Row 4
Row 5
Row 6
Row 7
Row 8
Row 9
Row 10
Row 11
Row 12
Row 13

Carol

**Thread pleater with 13 rows of cotton and pleat fabric.
Do not smock on rows 1 and 13.
Always centre the design.**

Ribbon Design

- Weave 5 mm double sided satin ribbon under the chevron design.

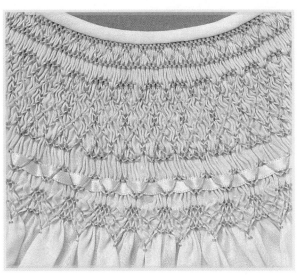

Coats Anchor Stranded Cotton		
No 050	Pink	
No 0203	Green	
No 0293	Yellow	
No 0129	Blue	
Berisford Ribbon		
No 70	Pale Pink	5 mm
Ribbon Lengths Required		
x 1 metre	Pale Pink	x 40 "

Fiona

Smocked on halfspace smocking rows.
Thread pleater with 15 halfspace rows of
cotton and pleat fabric.
Do not smock on rows 1 and 15.
Always centre the design.

Ribbon Design

- Weave 3 mm satin ribbon under the halfspace chevrons between rows 4 and 5, and 9 and 10.

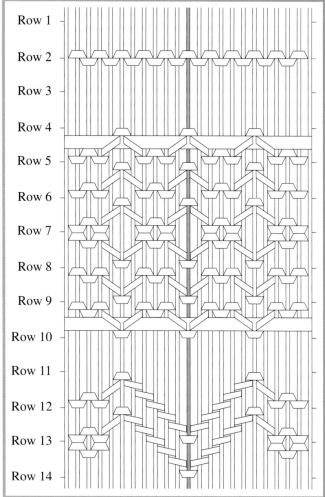

Row 1
Row 2
Row 3
Row 4
Row 5
Row 6
Row 7
Row 8
Row 9
Row 10
Row 11
Row 12
Row 13
Row 14

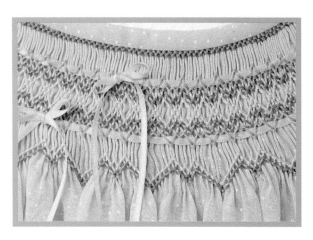

Coats Anchor Stranded Cotton		
No 050	Pink	
No 0205	Green	
No 0292	Yellow	
	Berisford Ribbon	
No 81	Jasmine	3 mm
	Ribbon Lengths Required	
x 2 metres	Jasmine	x 80 "

Michaela

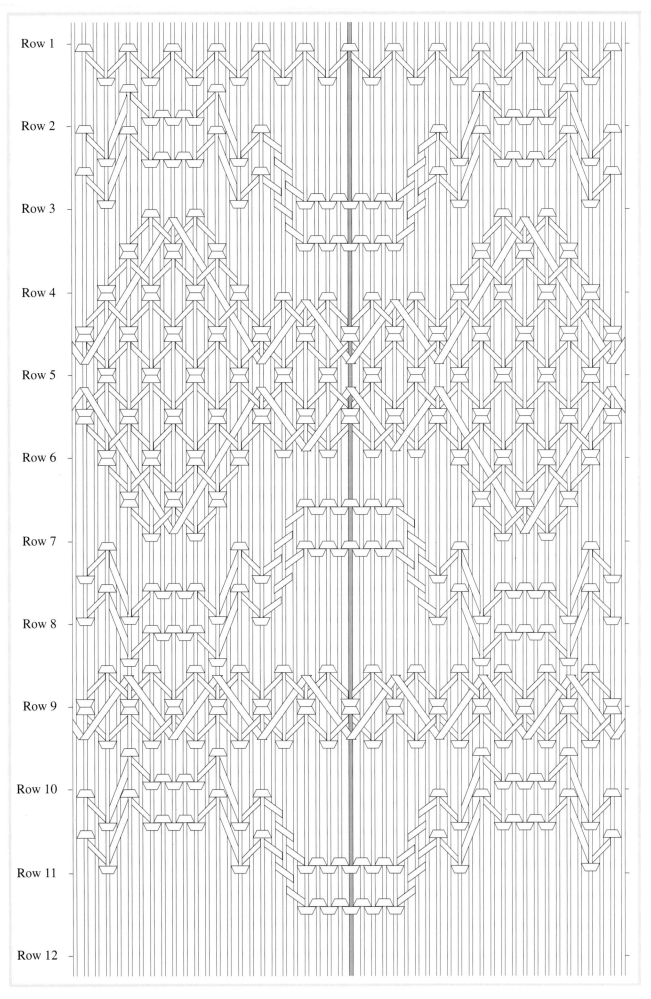

Row 1
Row 2
Row 3
Row 4
Row 5
Row 6
Row 7
Row 8
Row 9
Row 10
Row 11
Row 12

Michaela

Thread pleater with 19 rows of cotton
and pleat fabric.
Do not smock on rows 1 and 19.
Always centre the design.

Ribbon Design

- Start weaving at the centre of the chevron design
  according to the diagram.
- See *Zig Zag Weaving*, page 13.
- Mirror-image design from row 9 to row 18.

Coats Anchor Stranded Cotton

No 214	Green
No 042	Dark Pink
No 024	Pink
No 387	Cream

Berisford Ribbon

No 60	Dusky Pink	3 mm
No 275	Cream	3 mm

Ribbon Lengths Required
Double sided satin ribbon

x 50 cm	Dusky Pink	x 20 "	
x 2.25 metres	Cream	x 88 "	

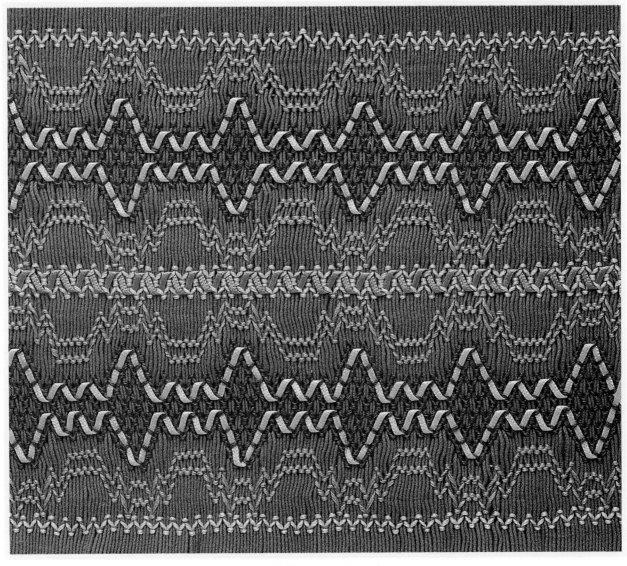

Smocked by Margie Prestedge

Caroline

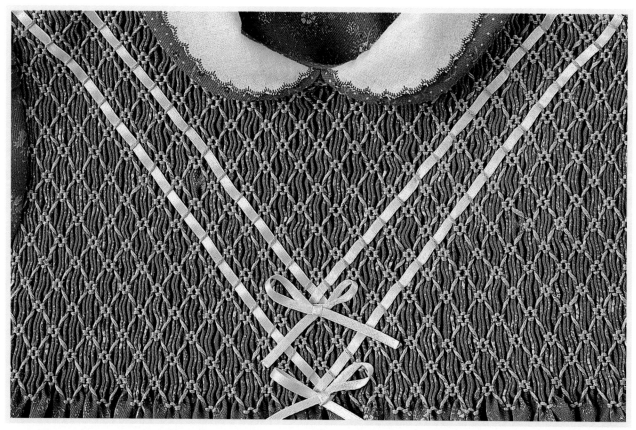

Smocked by Colleen Bowers

Thread pleater with 24 rows of cotton
and pleat fabric.
Do not smock on rows 1 and 24.
Always centre the design.

	Coats Anchor Stranded Cotton	
No 758	Peach	
	Berisford Ribbon	
No 275	Cream	3 mm
	Ribbon Lengths Required	
x 1.50 metres	Cream	x 60 "

Ribbon Design

- Start weaving at the centre of the design according to the photograph above.
- See *Diagonal Weaving*, page 15.
- Bows stitched separately.

Debbie

Smocked on halfspace smocking rows.
Thread pleater with 14 halfspace rows of cotton
and pleat fabric.
Do not smock on rows 1 and 14.
Always centre the design.

Ribbon Design

• See *Overlacing*, page 14.

• See *Overlacing*, page 14.

Coats Anchor Stranded Cotton		
No 024 & No 048	Pink	
No 0214	Green	
Berisford Ribbon		
No 220	Pink	3 mm
No 70	Pale Pink	1.5 mm
Ribbon Lengths Required		
x 1.25 metres	Pink & Pale Pink	x 50 "

Row 2

Row 4

Row 6

Row 8

Row 10

Row 12

Maria

Thread the pleater with 21 rows of cotton and pleat fabric.
Do not smock on rows 1 and 21.
Always centre the design.

Ribbon Design

- See *Ribbon Weaving*, page 10, and *Rope Weaving*, page 15.
- Backsmock rows 3 and 4, and 18 and 19, with cable stitch using 2 strands of embroidery cotton.
- Mirror-image design from row 11 to row 20.

Coats Anchor Stranded Cotton		
No 046	Red	
No 0228	Green	
Berisford Ribbon		
	Tartan ribbon	25 mm
No 23	Emerald	3 mm
Ribbon Lengths Required		
x 1 metre	Emerald	x 40 "
x 2 metre	Tartan ribbon,	x 80 "
	extended onto belt	

Maria

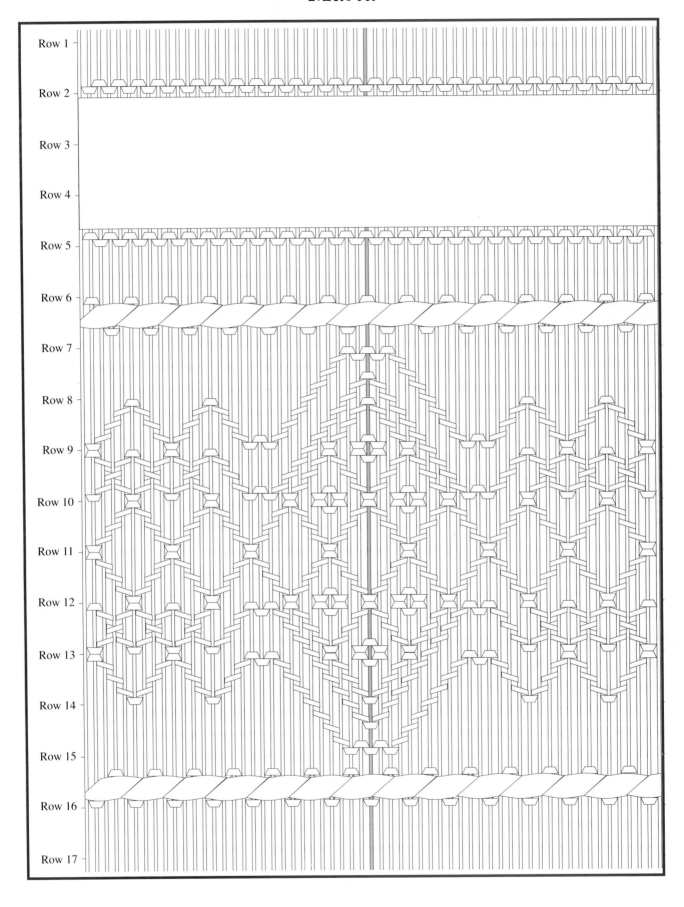

Nicola

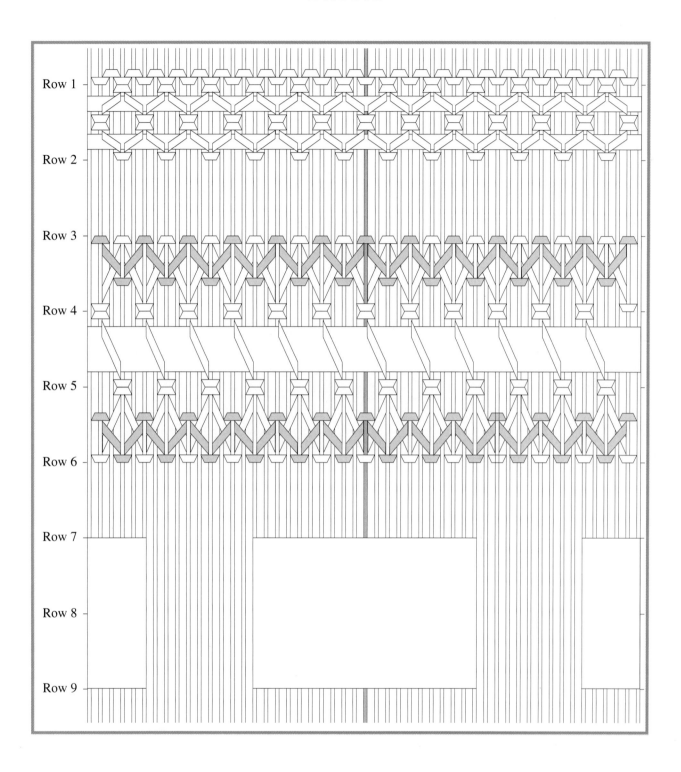

Row 1

Row 2

Row 3

Row 4

Row 5

Row 6

Row 7

Row 8

Row 9

65

Nicola

Thread pleater with 18 rows of cotton and pleat fabric.
Do not smock on rows 1 and 18.
Always centre the design.
See the *Rule of Three*, page 8

Ribbon Design

- See *Straight Lacing*, page 11, and *Ribbon Weaving: Buttonholes*, page 12.
- Ribbon is woven between rows 7 and 9.
- Skip 3 pleats and mark the valley of the next pleat with a vertical tacking thread.
- Working across from left to right, count 40 pleats, then 20 pleats from the first tacking thread; mark the valley. Continue across the row.
- Make 6 2.5 cm vertical buttonholes in the valleys.
- Backsmock between the buttonholes.
- Weave 25 mm Tartan ribbon through the buttonholes.
- Mirror-image design from row 8 to row 17.

Coats Anchor Stranded Cotton		
No 0217	Green	
No 0297	Yellow	
No 0127	Navy	
No 046	Red	

Berisford Ribbon		
No 24	Bottle	3 mm
No 15	Red	1.5 mm
No 13	Navy	1.5 mm
	Tartan	25 mm

Ribbon Lengths Required		
x 75 cm	Red, Navy & Bottle	x 30 "
x 40 cm	Tartan ribbon	x 16 "

Gemma

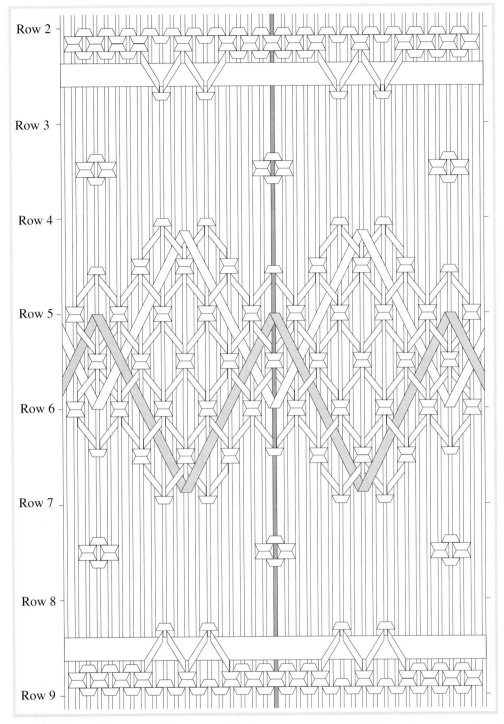

Row 2
Row 3
Row 4
Row 5
Row 6
Row 7
Row 8
Row 9

Thread pleater with 10 rows of cotton and pleat fabric. Do not smock on rows 1 and 10. Always centre the design.

Ribbon Design

- See *Straight Lacing*, page 11, and *Zig Zag Weaving*, page 13.
- Weave ribbon according to the diagram.

Coats Anchor Stranded Cotton

No 08   Apricot
No 0214 Green
No 0926 Cream

Berisford Ribbon

No   8   Apricot
         3 mm
No 275   Cream
         3 mm

Ribbon Lengths Required

Double sided satin ribbon
x 80 cm   Apricot
           x 32 "

Single sided satin ribbon
x 80 cm   Cream
           x 32 "

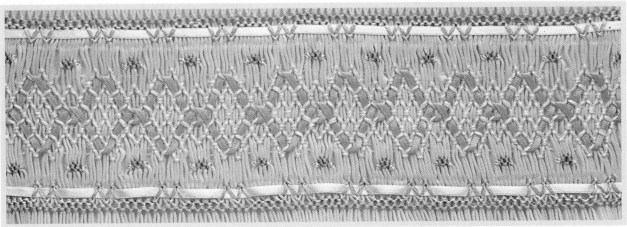

Tamlyn

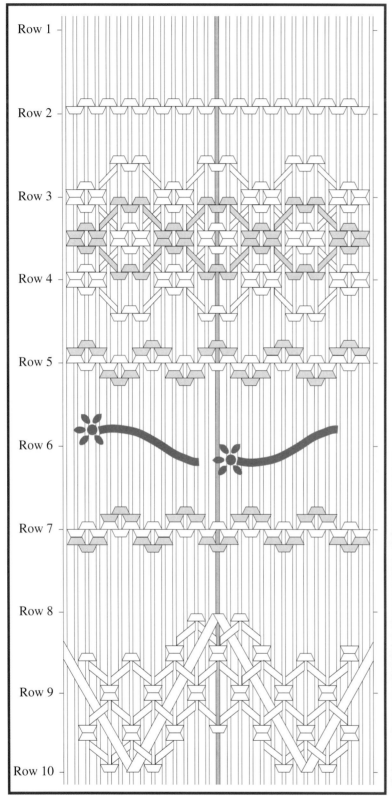

Row 1
Row 2
Row 3
Row 4
Row 5
Row 6
Row 7
Row 8
Row 9
Row 10

**Thread pleater with 11 rows of cotton and pleat fabric.
Do not smock on rows 1 and 11.
Always centre the design.**

Embroidery

- The design in the centre is a free form daisy chain, using Outline stitches for the stems and Lazy Daisy stitches for the flowers.
- Backsmock in cable stitch between rows 5, 6 and 7.

Ribbon Design

- Start weaving at the centre of the chevron design, according to the diagram.

Smocked by June Lippiat

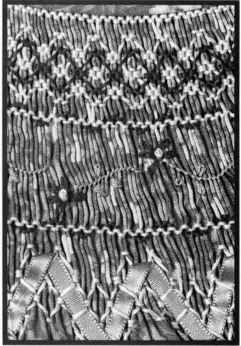

Coats Anchor Stranded Cotton		**Berisford Ribbon**	
		No 60 Dusky Pink	5 mm
No 0926	Cream		
No 069	Burgundy	**Ribbon Lengths Required**	
No 0208	Green	x 1.25 metres Double sided satin ribbon	x 50 "

Loryn

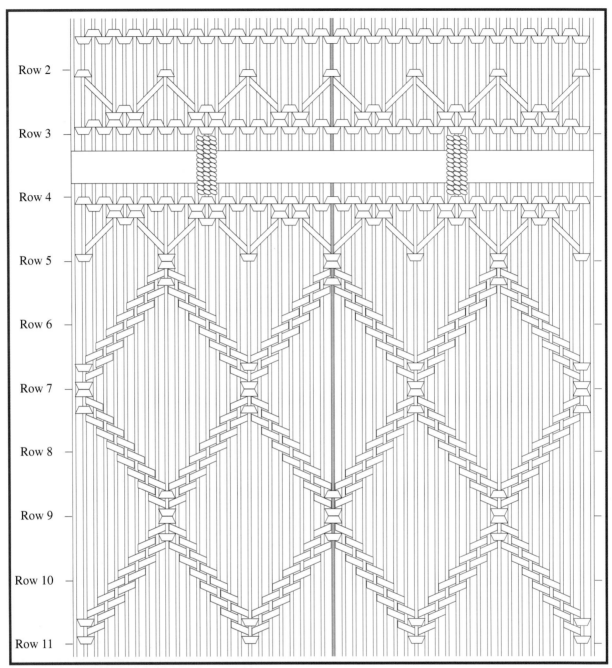

Row 2

Row 3

Row 4

Row 5

Row 6

Row 7

Row 8

Row 9

Row 10

Row 11

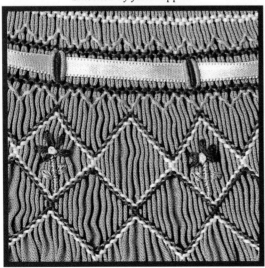

Smocked by June Lippiat

Coats Anchor Stranded Cotton
No 0926 Cream
No 069 Burgundy
No 0208 Green

Berisford Ribbon
No 275   Cream
5 mm

Ribbon Lengths Required
Single sided satin ribbon
x 50 cm Cream x 20 "

Thread pleater with 12 rows of cotton and pleat the fabric. Do not smock on rows 1 and 2. Always centre the design.

- Work bullion rosebuds in 3 strands of embroidery cotton, 15 wraps for each knot. Use 2 different shades of cotton.
- Start the bullion rosebud on a cable stitch.

Ribbon Design

- Weave ribbon under each bullion rosebud.

Francesca

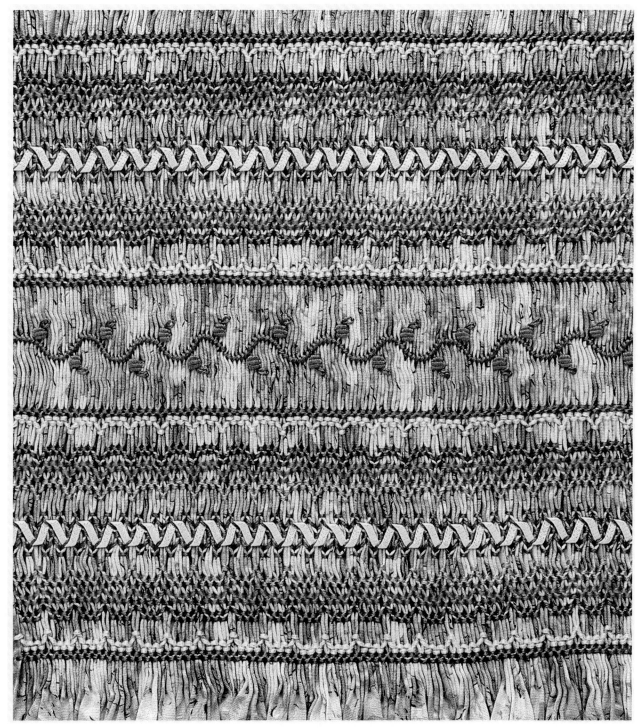

Smocked by Sheila Bennett

Francesca

**Thread pleater with 21 rows of cotton and pleat fabric.
Do not smock on rows 1 and 21.
Always centre the design.**

Trailing Vine

- Vertically aligned with the rest of the design.
- Occupies half a space, and extends a quarter space above and a quarter space below row 10.
- Begin the trailing vine on row 10 and smock 3 Outline stitches up a quarter of a space. Then smock 3 Outline stitches across and 5 Outline stitches down to a quarter of a space below row 10. Smock 3 Outline stitches across and then 5 Outline stitches up to a quarter of a space above row 10. Continue across the row in this way.

- Backsmock rows 9, 10 and 11.
- Mirror-image design between row 10 and row 20.
- Use 2 strands of pink thread (6/8/6 wraps) for bullion rosebuds.
- Use 2 strands of dark green thread for leaves.

Ribbon Design

- Zig Zag Weaving according to the diagram.
- See *Zig Zag Weaving*, page 13.

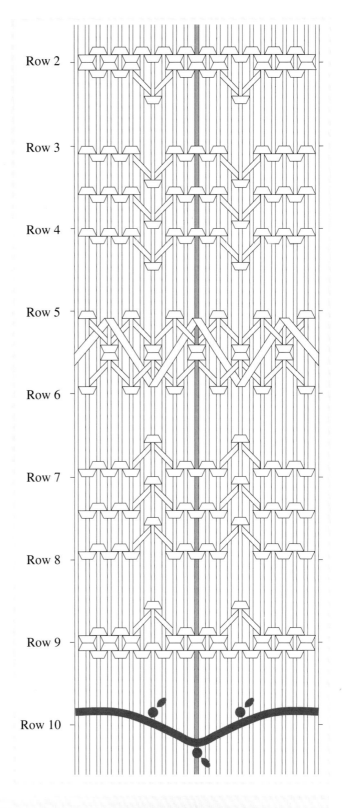

Row 2

Row 3

Row 4

Row 5

Row 6

Row 7

Row 8

Row 9

Row 10

Coats Anchor Stranded Cotton	
No 888	Pink
No 301	Yellow
No 878	Dark Green
No 875	Light Green

Berisford Ribbon		
No 63	Maize	3 mm

Ribbon Lengths Required
Double sided satin ribbon

x 1 metre	Maize	x 40 "

Genevieve

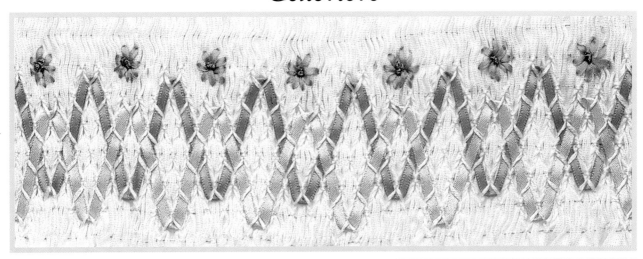

Thread pleater with 24 rows of cotton and pleat fabric.
Do not smock on row 1.
Always centre the design.

- Backsmock rows 2 to 18 with 3-step Trellis diamonds, using 2 strands of embroidery cotton.
- Use silk ribbon for flowers.

Ribbon Design

- See *Zig Zag Weaving*, page 13.
- Weave ribbon according to the diagram.

Coats Anchor Stranded Cotton		
No 01	White	
Liberty Ribbon		
	Liberty Ribbon	25 mm
No 52	Hot Pink	3 mm
No 78	Aqua	3 mm
Silk Ribbon		
x 2 metres	Pink	2 mm
Ribbon Lengths Required		
x 1 metre	Liberty Ribbon	x 40 "
x 4 metres	Hot Pink	x 160 "
x 3 metres	Aqua	x 120 "

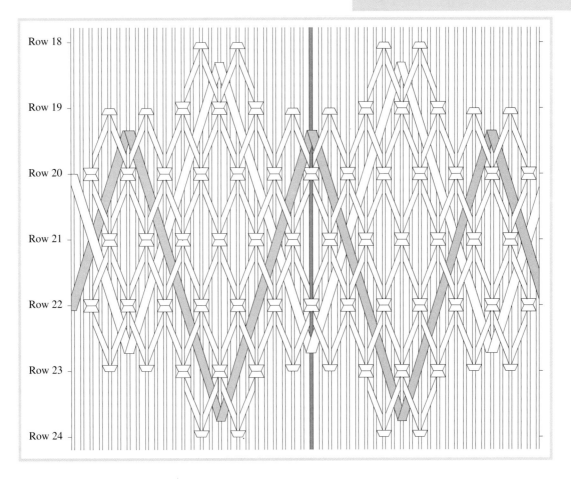

Ashleigh

Smocked by Lea Dandridge

Thread pleater with 9 rows of cotton and pleat fabric.
Do not smock on rows 1 and 9.
Always centre the design.

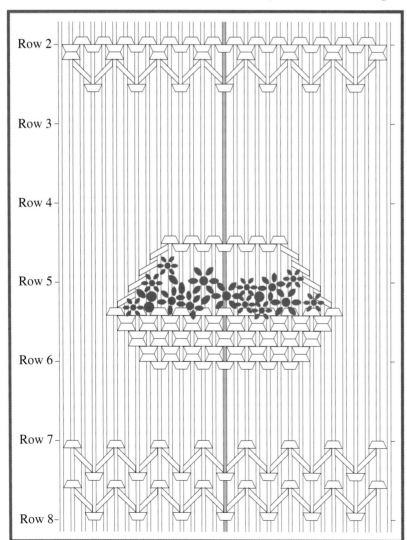

- Backsmock rows 3 and 4, and between the baskets on rows 4, 5 and 6, using 2 strands of embroidery cotton.

Basket

- Basket is worked in blue silk ribbon according to the diagram.
- Start working basket on row 6 using 15 cable stitches.
- Smocking and embroidery stitches worked in silk ribbon, using Lazy Daisy, French knots and Stem stitch.

Coats Anchor Stranded Cotton
Colour to match background of fabric

Silk Ribbon
Yellow, Red, Pink & Blue   4 mm

Ribbon Lengths Required
x 3 metres   Yellow, Red, Pink
x 120 "   & Blue

Tracy

Smocked by Lea Dandridge

Row 2

Row 3

Row 4

Row 5

Row 6

Row 7

Row 8

Row 9

**Thread pleater with 10 rows
of cotton and pleat fabric.
Do not smock on
rows 1 and 10.
Always centre the design.**

Ribbon Design

- Backsmock rows 3 to 8,
  using 2 strands of
  embroidery cotton.
- Work free style embroidery
  using Lazy Daisy, French
  knots and Stem stitch.
- Work embroidery stitches
  with silk ribbon.
- See *Uses of Ribbon*, page 4.

*Coats Anchor Stranded
Cotton*
Colour to match background
of fabric

Ribbon
Colours to match the floral
fabric of your choice

Chiara

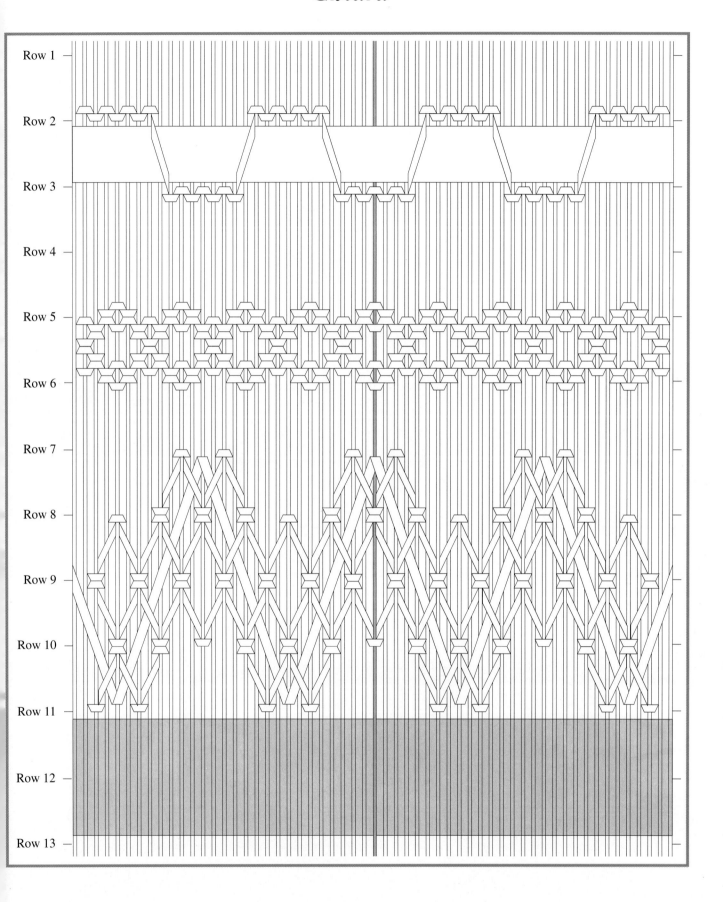

Row 1

Row 2

Row 3

Row 4

Row 5

Row 6

Row 7

Row 8

Row 9

Row 10

Row 11

Row 12

Row 13

Chiara

**Thread pleater with 22 rows of cotton
and pleat fabric.
Do not smock on rows 1 and 22.
Always centre the design.**

Ribbon Design

- See *Ribbon Weaving*, page 10, *Straight Lacing*,
  page 11 and *Zig Zag Weaving*, page 13.
- Sew the ribbon to the fabric between rows 11
  and 13, *before* pleating the fabric.
- Lengthen stitches between rows 2 and 3,
  and rows 20 and 21, to accommodate the
  ribbon.

Coats Anchor Stranded Cotton		
No 0230	Green	
No 0150	Navy	
Berisford Ribbon		
	Tartan ribbon	25 mm
	Tartan ribbon	15 mm
No 24	Bottle	3 mm
Ribbon Lengths Required		
x 1.6 metres	Tartan ribbon	x 63 "
x 1.5 metres	Bottle	x 59 "
x 1.8 metres	Skirt	x 71 "

Leigh-Anne

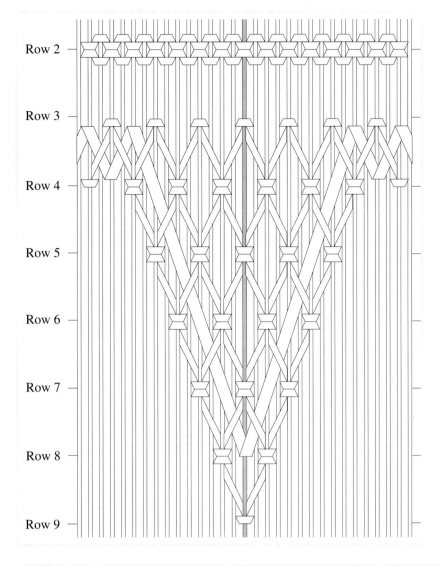

Row 2
Row 3
Row 4
Row 5
Row 6
Row 7
Row 8
Row 9

Thread pleater with 10 rows
of cotton and pleat fabric.
Do not smock on rows 1
and 10.
Always centre the design.

Ribbon Design

- Weave ribbon according to the
  diagram.

Coats Anchor
Stranded Cotton
No 0292   Yellow

Berisford Ribbon
No   63   Maize   3 mm

Ribbon Lengths Required
Double sided satin ribbon
x 1.50 metres   Maize   x 59 "

Fabia

Thread pleater with 9 rows of cotton and pleat fabric.
Do not smock on rows 1 and 9.
Always centre the design.

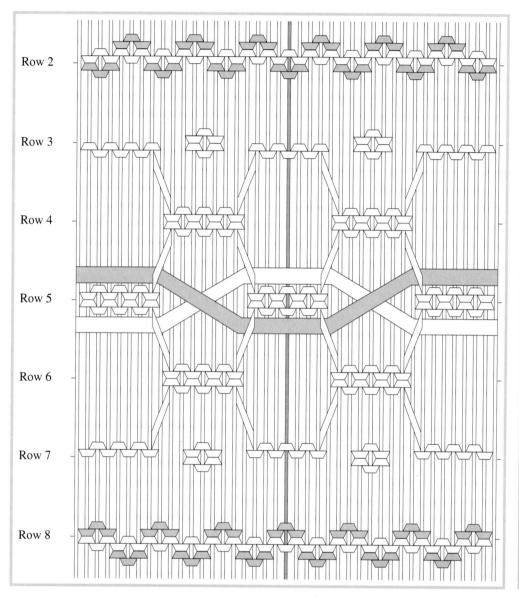

Row 2

Row 3

Row 4

Row 5

Row 6

Row 7

Row 8

Ribbon Design

- Weave ribbon using 2 colours, according to the diagram.
- Ribbon forms a design around the stitches.

Coats Anchor Stranded Cotton
No 01   White
No 0214   Green

Berisford Ribbon
No 1   White
          3 mm
No 76 Cornflower
          3 mm

Ribbon Lengths Required
x 1 metre   White
x 1 metre   Blue
          x 40 "

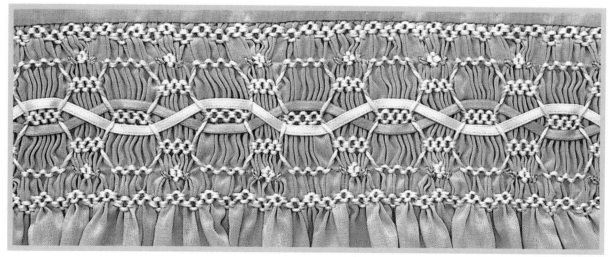

Lynne

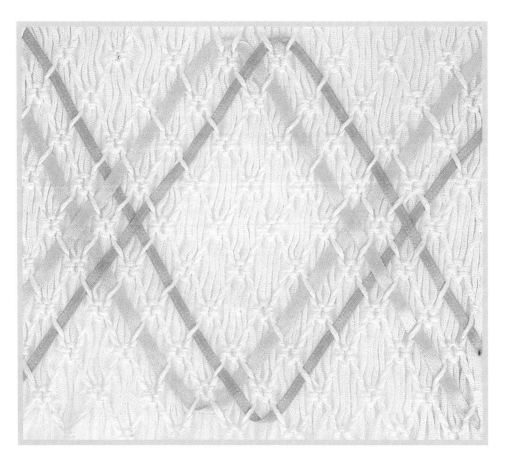

**Thread pleater with 13 rows of cotton and pleat fabric.
Do not smock on rows 1 and 13.
Always centre the design.**

Coats Anchor Stranded Cotton
No 01   White

Berisford Ribbon
No 71   Peach   3 mm
No 08   Apricot   1.5 mm

Ribbon Lengths Required
Double sided satin ribbon
x 1.5 metres   Peach   x 59 "
x 1.5 metres   Apricot   x 59"

Ribbon Design

- Weave ribbon according to the diagram.
- See *Diagonal Weaving*, page 15.

Chiara

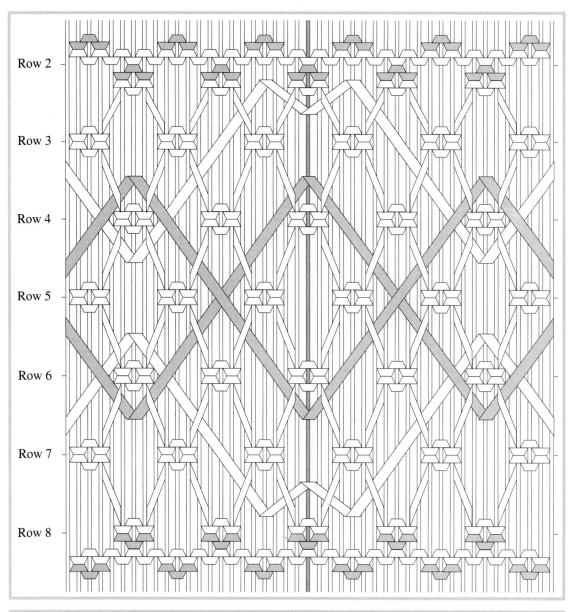

Row 2

Row 3

Row 4

Row 5

Row 6

Row 7

Row 8

Coats Anchor Stranded Cotton
No 050   Pink
No   01   White
No 0186   Turquoise

Berisford Ribbon
No 2   Pink   3 mm
No 1   White   3 mm

Ribbon Lengths Required
Double sided satin ribbon
x 2 metres · Pink & White   x 80 "

**Thread pleater with 21 rows of cotton
and pleat fabric.
Do not smock on rows 1 and 21.
Always centre the design.**

Ribbon Design

- See *Overlacing*, page 14.
- Weave according to the diagram.

90

Flowers

- Backsmock between rows 9 and 13 using cable stitch with 2 strands of embroidery cotton.
- Work flowers according to the graph, using 6 strands of embroidery cotton.
- Start the centre cable flowerette first.
- Leaves and stems are worked in outline stitch.

Cushions to Dream On

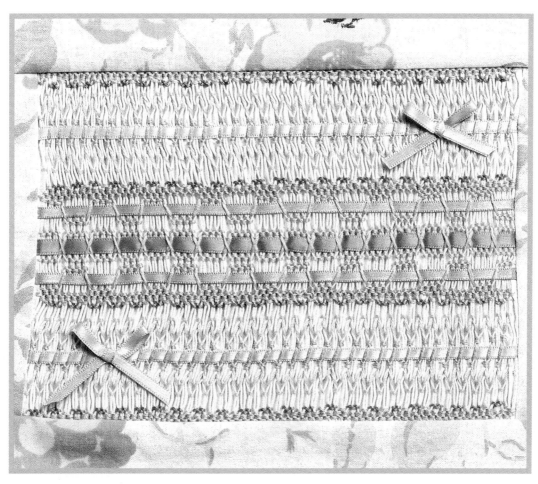

About the Author

Madeline Bird has been smocking for 18 years. Inspired by her mother, an expert seamstress, she now continues the family tradition by creating beautifully smocked garments for her two daughters. Madeline has taught smocking for twelve years. She is a founder member and Chairlady of the Cape Smocker's Guild, which has a membership of 180. Madeline runs a mail order business called Smickety Smocks, for which she has co-designed and printed eight children's, and three adult's dress patterns for smocking. She has contributed several articles on smocking to various women's magazines and has also travelled extensively, including a trip to Australia to lecture on ribbon smocking.